The GREATEST
in the WORLD

illustrated by
Graham Kennedy

Joe Inglis

The Greatest
Dog
Tips in the World

A 'The Greatest in the World' book

www.thegreatestintheworld.com

Illustrations:
Graham Kennedy
gkillus@aol.com

Cover & layout design:
The designcouch
www.designcouch.co.uk

Cover images: © www.morguefile.com, © Carina Hansen;
© Leah-Anne Thompson; both courtesy of www.fotolia.com,
© Clive Nichols

Copy editor:
Bronwyn Robertson
www.theartsva.com

Series creator/editor: Steve Brookes

First published in 2006 by Public Eye Publications

This edition published in 2007 by
The Greatest in the World Ltd., PO Box 3182
Stratford-upon-Avon, Warwickshire CV37 7XW

Text and Illustrations Copyright © 2007 – The Greatest in the World Ltd.

A CIP catalogue record for this book is available from the British Library
ISBN 978-1-905151-67-7

Printed and bound in China by 1010 Printing International Ltd.

To my wonderful wife Jenny
for all her love and support.

Contents

Introduction

Writing a book of dog tips sounded like a pretty straightforward assignment – after all, I've been a vet for nearly ten years, and before that I spent five years learning everything there is to know about the inner workings of dogs at Bristol vet school. However, when I sat down in front of my computer and pondered the task in front of me, every idea I had for a useful tip seemed to come from elsewhere – I was never taught at vet school that garlic keeps fleas away, or that feeding cotton wool can save a dog's life. Instead, I found myself drawing on all the experiences I've had with dogs since I qualified, from dealing with patients at the surgery to bringing up my lovely two collie crosses at home.

From carrying Pan and Badger home from the farm in Devon where they came from, to losing them repeatedly on Cleeve Hill in Cheltenham, my experiences as a 'father' to these wonderful dogs have had far more influence on the tips you're about to read than my veterinary training ever did. Of course there is plenty of good vet science in these pages, but I hope I've also managed to convey the truly personal nature of dog ownership. This book is not meant as a comprehensive encyclopaedia of dog knowledge – think of it more as a guidebook to help you negotiate the sometimes tricky path of dog ownership.

Dip into it as you feel the urge or the need, and take on board the tips that apply to you and your dog — but above all, never forget that you and your dog are a special team and there's very little that good old common sense and TLC won't sort out!

Good luck!

Joe

"I think dogs are the most amazing creatures; they give unconditional love. For me they are the role model for being alive. "

Gilda Radner

A new dog?

chapter 1
A new dog?

Bringing a new dog into your life and home requires plenty of planning and dedication, be it a little puppy or a full-grown adult. Getting it wrong can be a disaster for you and for your new best friend, so here are a few tips to point you in the right direction.

Are you ready for a dog?

So you're thinking about getting a dog? Perhaps it will be your first ever pet or maybe the new arrival will need to fit into a busy family of animals. Whatever your situation, you need to do some serious thinking before committing yourself—and your new dog—to a life together. Don't forget the truth behind the old saying "a dog is for life, not just for Christmas". Dogs can live for twenty years or more, so make sure you're ready to share your life for the foreseeable future!

DID YOU KNOW ... ?

That Basset Hounds can't swim – their legs are too short and their bodies too long. So if you live by a river and want a dog who will love splashing around in the water, take Basset hounds off your list!

Is your house ready for a dog?

Owning a dog is more than just walks in the park and dog bowls in the kitchen. If you take a dog into your life you need to make sure your house is a suitable home for your new canine companion – and also consider how sharing your home with a dog will change things for you and your family. Are you ready to say goodbye to spotless sofas and clean carpets and say hello to muddy paw-prints and furry furniture? Are you ready to give up a perfectly manicured flowerbed in exchange for a well-dug doggy garden?

If you're not sure, why not pay a visit to some friends who have a dog? If you find yourself perched uncomfortably on the sofa picking dog hairs off your trousers, maybe a dog isn't for you. But if the sight of Fido demolishing your friends' daffodils or weeing in their wisteria leaves you relaxed, it's time to start thinking about which dog will suit you best!

Puppy love?

When most people take on a new dog, it's usually a puppy. Sharing those early weeks and months, when the puppy is a bundle of cute, cuddly fun, is a wonderful experience, and interacting with an animal at this age is the best way to make a really strong, life-long bond.

However, getting a puppy is not your only option. Many people prefer to take on an older dog, either from a friend or a rescue centre. Maybe you don't want the hassle of training a boisterous new puppy, or perhaps you're elderly and don't feel it's fair to take on a young dog. But whatever your circumstances, it's well worth considering an adult dog, especially when you consider how many languish, unloved in rescue centres. Giving one of these abandoned dogs a new home and a new life can be just as rewarding as taking on a puppy.

RACE TIP!

Just a quick idea – if you're thinking of taking on an adult dog, why not consider a rescue greyhound. There are literally hundreds of these dogs looking for homes every year after their racing careers finish, and they make wonderful, gentle pets.

Westie or Wolfhound?

How do you go about choosing the right dog for you? After all, there are hundreds of different breeds, from giants like Afghan Hounds to tiny terriers like the Jack Russell, not to mention the infinite variety of cross breeds that come in almost every shape, size and temperament.

To choose the best dog for you, my tip is to start by narrowing your choice down. Do you want a big dog or a little one, a manic mutt or a passive pet, a long-haired dog or a short-haired one? And think about why you are getting a dog. If you would like to show or breed, then think about a pedigree dog, if not, a cross-breed might suit you best. And then, do your research. Read up about the breeds you're interested in to find out about their character, their potential pitfalls, and decide which one best suits your lifestyle.

Meet 'n greet

The best way to really find out which breed is for you is to get out there and meet them – visit friends or breeders who own them, or spend an afternoon at the local rescue kennels. And don't forget dog shows, where you can chat to hundreds of breeders and enthusiasts and really find out whether it's a Poodle or a Papillion, a mongrel or a Manchester Terrier that's the one for you.

Small is beautiful

If you don't live in a big house, or have a big garden, why not think about getting a terrier. They can be great companions and have wonderful personalities. My favourites are Jack Russells which are very tough and loyal, and don't need as much exercise as many big dogs.

Bigger isn't always better

Lots of people love big dogs, whether as a status symbol, or for reassurance on night-time walks. There are lots of big breeds out there, from Wolfhounds to Mastiffs, but only consider taking one on if you've got the room and energy they require. Bigger dogs need more exercise and attention, and won't be happy cooped up in a tiny flat or house all day. They also tend to have shorter life spans than smaller dogs – in some cases the average life-expectancy can be as short as 7 or 8 years.

And the final thing to remember is the bigger the dog, the bigger the bills. Everything, from food to vet bills, will be more expensive for a large dog, so make sure you can afford the dog of your dreams before you take him on.

Joe's top five breeds

Here are my personal favourites in the doggy world:

1. **Border Collie**
   The most intelligent dogs around, these lithe, energetic dogs, originally from the Scottish borders, can be a real handful but no other breed can match them for brains and instincts. Only for those with plenty of time, energy and space!

2. **Labrador**
   The opposite of the collie in terms of temperament— quiet, dependable and sensitive—Labradors are the ultimate family companions.

3. **Jack Russell terrier**
   Bred by the Reverend Jack Russell in the 19th century as a pocket-sized fox hound, the Jack Russell makes up in character what he lacks in size!

4. **Beagle**
   One of the happiest breeds around, combining good looks with a friendly temperament and unusual longevity. Watch out for his voice though, as they can get a bit noisy if left alone.

5. **Mongrel!**
   I know it's not a breed, but some of the finest dogs around have lots of mixed blood. It gives them plenty of so-called 'hybrid vigour' and they are much less prone to inherited diseases than many purebred dogs.

" There is no
psychiatrist in the
world like a puppy
licking your face. "

Bern Williams

How much is that doggy in the window?

Once you've decided on a breed or type of dog, now it's time to find him or her. But how exactly do you search out your perfect pooch?

There are many different places to look. If you're thinking about an older dog, or taking on a rescued puppy, then you should head straight down to your local animal rescue centre. If a pedigree puppy is going to be your perfect partner then try the Kennel Club who will be able to give you names and numbers for local breeders. And what about paying a visit to your vet, who will know of any new litters on the way, and any dogs needing new homes? Try to avoid pet shops and puppy farms, as the puppies they rear and sell are often unhealthy and poorly treated.

Quick tip

BEWARE THE DODGY DOGGY DEALER

Never, ever buy a puppy without seeing where it was brought up and meeting its mother (and father if possible). Some unscrupulous breeders and puppy farmers will try to get you to meet them somewhere such as a service station to hand over the puppy. Always say no to this – if they won't let you see their breeding establishment, it's usually because it's not up to standard and the puppy has been reared in terrible conditions.

Litter louts!

You've chosen your breed, found a breeder, and now the big day has finally come — it's time to pick out the puppy who will share your life. But when you're confronted with a basket of adorable puppies, how do you pick the right one? Should you pick the biggest pup in the litter? Or the most friendly? Or the cutest?

Well, there are a few key things to look for when you're making your choice. Firstly, avoid puppies which are much smaller than the others. Very small puppies often don't thrive as well as their bigger brothers and sisters, and might be more prone to health problems later in life.

Then think about the character of the pup you want. If you want a bold, dominant dog, pick out the big fat pup that comes charging straight over to you. But if you would prefer a more laid back dog, look for the relaxed pup in the middle of the crowd.

But most of all let your heart rule your head, and pick the pup you fall in love with. At the end of the day, bonding with your new dog is far more important than how he looks!

DID YOU KNOW ... ?
Scientists have discovered that dogs can smell the presence of autism in children.

'Seizure Alert' dogs can alert their owners up to an hour before the onset of an epileptic seizure.

It's all in the timing

Before you pick up your new pup and rush her home, make sure she's the right age. Bitches will usually wean their puppies at between 5 and 7 weeks of age, and it's vital not to take puppies before this. If you take them too young, they might miss out on vital antibodies and nutrients that they get from their mother's milk. On the other hand, leave them with their mother too long and you risk other kinds of problems. Dogs are most receptive to socialisation and bonding between 8 weeks and 16 weeks, and so it's vital your new dog is getting used to you and your home in this period.

So, the best time to take a puppy is between 7 and 10 weeks, thereby ensuring that they get all the protection their mother's milk can offer, whilst being young enough to make that all-important bond with you and your family.

Quick tip

A HOUSE FIT FOR A NEW HOUND

Bringing home a new puppy is a big moment and you want to make sure your new pup feels safe and comfortable in his new surroundings. Make sure there's a new, clean dog bed waiting for him, as well as a full water bowl and a few toys to play with.

If you've got other pets, it's worth keeping them out of the way while the new arrival finds his feet for an hour or two. Put the cat out or take the dog for a walk, and if the kids are going to be over-excited, maybe take them out for a walk too!

Happiness is a warm puppy.

Charles M Schulz

The first month

chapter 2
The first month

Making the right decisions about taking on a new dog is just the start. Now you've got your puppy home, the real hard work begins. Here are some helpful tips to help you avoid making a right dog's dinner of your first few weeks together!

Opening night

With your new pup safely asleep on her bed, a nice meal of puppy food inside her and a contented look on her face, you sneak out of the kitchen and off to your own bed. You close your eyes and drift off, dreaming of happy puppies and country walks. But then you are suddenly awoken by a horrible, piercing cry of anguish, which seems to fill the whole house. You jump out of bed and rush to see what calamity could have befallen your precious puppy.

It's nothing serious, just a case of first night nerves. She is looking up at you from her basket with those sad 'please don't leave me down here' eyes. So you don't. Instead you decide to let her have just this one night in your bed. From tomorrow night onwards you will be really firm, but look at her, poor thing. You pick her up and take her back upstairs where she curls up happily next to you and everyone sleeps happily.

So, did you make the right decision? Read on ...

Isn't that how it works? … Wrong!

If you take this approach, prepare yourself to either share your bed with your dog for the rest of its life, or to put up with a howling puppy for many months to come. The only solution is to be firm from day one, and teach your puppy that howling brings no reward. Endure one long night of howling without returning to comfort your puppy and she will never try it again. If you give in at 3am, she'll be sure to try the same tactic the next night – only this time she knows she might have to persist until at least the same time again. It might sound harsh, but dog training is all about being firm and fair. Lay down your ground rules from day one, and you'll have a happy, well-behaved dog – and neighbours who still talk to you!

It's always doggy dinner time

When you have a new puppy, you take over from his mother, and take on the responsibility for making sure he eats the right amount of the right food. Get this wrong, and it could affect your dog for the rest of his life.

The most important thing about feeding puppies is to offer them lots of meals. With their mother, they will have been feeding every three or four hours, so you need to feed a puppy at least four times a day when they are seven or eight weeks old. As time goes by you can gradually reduce the number of feeds, down to two by the time they are about three months old.

Quick tip

GRUB'S UP!

There are many different dogs foods out there, but whichever one you choose, make sure it's suitable for puppies, as they have special nutritional requirements. It's best to offer a mixture of wet and dried foods, and feed the amount stated on the packaging – too much food at this age could lead to an overweight adult, and even cause serious health problems like arthritis.

Cereal is for children

Lots of breeders will arm you with pages of strict instructions on how to feed your new puppy – cold porridge and Weetabix in the morning followed by buttered toast and a cup of tea at exactly 11.30 a.m. and so on. My advice is to use those pages to line the kitchen floor, and stick to feeding your puppy a sensible diet of proper puppy food!

Weaned puppies have no need for milk, and it can cause stomach upsets, as can many human foods like butter, toast and cereals. While it's fine to listen to your breeder when it comes to choosing a suitable brand of pet food (it's often best to stick to the one they have been using), don't be pressured into sticking to strange routines and unsuitable diets – and remember, what suits you or your children, won't necessarily suit your dog.

Oops!

It's the first morning with your new puppy, and you walk into the kitchen to find a pile of pooh, a puddle of wee, and an apologetic-looking pup. Should you ...

a) shout at the puppy and rub their nose in the mess,

b) ignore the problem and clean everything up, or

c) let your puppy straight out into the garden or yard and praise them when they do their business outside?

The answer is, of course, **c)**. Toilet training is all about positive reinforcement and encouragement, rather than punishment. Dogs, like all animals, are naturally clean, and nearly all dogs will get the hang of toilet training very quickly given the right help and encouragement. Simply take your puppy into the garden at regular intervals and praise him whenever he goes to the toilet outside.

What's black and white and peed all over?

Newspaper of course! Lots of people still use newspaper as a way of house training puppies and while it can help soak up some of the mess, it can delay the training process because it encourages the puppy to think it's okay to wee in the house – and on your papers. It's much better to whisk the puppy out into the garden at the first hint that he is about to go for a wee, and reward him with a titbit when he's just finished doing his business outside. It's also a good idea to take him out straight after he's eaten because this is when he's likely to want to go to the toilet.

Top dog wins

Play is also important for establishing the dominance order in your family, and it's important that she knows you and all the family are the top dogs. To do this, make sure you win any games like tug-of-war, and that you start and finish any games you play. By establishing that you are in charge, she's much more likely to grow up knowing her place and be well-behaved and content.

Quick tip

EASY DOES IT!
Just a quick reminder not to be too rough with your new puppy, especially when playing tug of war. At this young age their jaws will be weak and can be damaged if you play too violently with them. Instead of wrenching the toy out of his mouth, teach him to drop it on command by offering a nice treat. As well as keeping his jaw in one piece, teaching him to drop is a really useful command – and one you could be very thankful for in later years when he's busy chewing your best slippers!

Clean it up

If (well, when) your puppy has an accident in the house, it's important to clean it up straight away with a good cleaner specially designed to take the smell away. Most normal household cleaners won't get rid of the smell entirely, and any odour that lingers will encourage the puppy to wee in that spot again. Use a special anti-odour cleaner from your pet shop or vet because this will get rid of the smell completely every time.

Puppy power!

A young puppy should be full of energy and enthusiasm for life, and needs plenty of entertainment to keep her fit and happy. Make sure you've got a few robust toys for her to play with, as games are a vital part of learning behavioural skills for a puppy, and spend as much time with her as you can. This will build up that bond between you and will also make sure she doesn't get bored — bored puppies turn into badly behaved dogs.

A visit to the vet

Within the first week of having your new puppy, it's well worth a trip to your vet to have a check up and find out about vaccinations, worming and all the other important topics you need to know about. Most vets will offer this introductory check up free of charge.

If you've not been to a vet before, ask friends with dogs for their recommendation, and go to see a few practices before settling on the one you feel most comfortable with. It's important to establish a good relationship with your vet, so choose one where you and your new puppy are made to feel welcome.

DID YOU KNOW ... ?
Pharaoh Hounds are the only dogs that blush. They do this when they are excited or happy; and their ears, nose and eyes become pink.

Puppy love

- A puppy is born blind, deaf and toothless.

- During its first week 90% of a puppy's time is spent sleeping and 10% eating.

- A puppy is only able to crawl during its first week.

- A puppy begins to see when it is between 2 to 3 weeks old.

- During the ages of 3 to 7 weeks a puppy's first teeth, or milk teeth, will appear.

- At the age of 3 weeks a puppy will develop its sense of smell.

- A puppy will sleep for 14 hours every day.

- A puppy's adult teeth start to come through between 4 and 8 months when it starts to chew everything!

- Some puppies reach sexual maturity at the age of eight months.

- A puppy is considered and adult at the age of one year. At this age it is as physically as mature as a 15 year-old human.

- Bulldog puppies are delivered by caesarean section because of their large heads.

My top tips for choosing a good vet

1. Small practices tend to be friendlier and it's easier to always see the same vet.

2. Out of hours in house – lots of vets have a dedicated out of hours service but this will cost you a lot of money if you have to use it, and you won't be dealing with your own vet.

3. Big new premises are all very well but don't forget that your fees are paying for it, and many of these big super practices have to charge a lot more than smaller practices as a result.

4. Parking is vital. This might sound like a minor point, but when you've got a sick dog the last thing you want is to spend hours looking for a parking place.

5. Make an appointment to meet the veterinarian as well as the staff. How do they interact with customers as well as each other? Ask for a tour of the facility. It would be a good idea to not ask for the tour in advance. This way you can see how the facility is kept without being warned of a visitor.

6. Look for cleanliness especially in the kennel area. If you see unclean kennels it might mean they do not have enough staff to care for the animals. Hygiene is important due to the spread of diseases among animals.

7. Ask about emergency care? Is it even offered? Accidents can happen to your pet at anytime. Is there 24/7 emergency pet care? Find out if your dog does have to stay overnight, will there be a member of staff staying with him?

8. Trust your dog! A good vet should treat your dog with care and affection and your dog is the best person to let you know how good your vet is in this area.

Don't look – it's injection time!

One of the most vital parts of looking after a new puppy is to have him vaccinated. This protects him against some really nasty diseases, including distemper, parvovirus and leptospirosis. Not long ago, before most dogs were routinely vaccinated, these diseases killed thousands of animals every year, so they really are an essential part of looking after your new friend.

The injections themselves are very small, and generally painless. Most vets will put the needle into the scruff, and this part of the skin is not at all sensitive to pain as it is where bitches pick up their puppies using their teeth.

The first injection should be given when your puppy is about eight weeks old, and the second two to four weeks later. Full protection comes a week after the second jab, so it's worth keeping away from parks and other communal spaces until then.

A flea circus!

Not sure if your lovely new puppy has got fleas? Well here's a tip to help you find out.

Take a sheet of white paper, and then use a fine comb to go through your puppy's fur, especially along his back. Comb onto the piece of paper, and collect whatever comes out of the coat. If you find lots of tiny black specks, this could be flea dirt. To check, dab the specks with a piece of wet cotton wool. If it is flea dirt, the cotton wool will get stained red thanks to the blood in the dirt. If your puppy does have fleas, get your vet to prescribe some spray or drops – and you might also need to spray the house if it's a bad infestation.

What about worms?

Having a living, wriggling worm inside your tummy sounds pretty horrible, but the truth is that nearly all puppies will have some worms inside them. They are often infected with worms straight from their mother, through the milk and even via the blood before they are born!

These worms can make your puppy ill if not sorted out, and they can also be a risk to human health, especially children. To prevent any problems, make sure children don't come into contact with any dog faeces, and try to stop them being licked on the face by puppies (harder than it sounds, I know!).

When you get your puppy, check that it has been wormed with a good wormer at least twice, and then you need to worm her every two weeks until she is three months old.

A chip in the neck saves lives

Thousands of dogs are lost and stolen every year, and getting them back can be almost impossible, because it's often your word against the new 'owner's'. However, my next tip is a really effective way of making sure your new puppy is always identified as your dog.

What you need to do is have a tiny microchip implanted in his neck. This contains a unique number which is held, along with your details, on a national database. Your vet can implant the chip using a needle (really don't look at this one – it's pretty big!) and once it's in place, it's there for life, and can be easily read using a special scanner.

DNA – the ultimate identification

Not satisfied with just a microchip? Well if you want the ultimate in dog protection you could consider signing up to a new service with a company called the Missing Pets Bureau (**www.missingpetsbureau.com**). They take a DNA swab from your dog's mouth and this can be used to prove the identity of your dog in a court of law. The bureau will also hunt down your dog if it goes missing, so if you've got a very valuable (or just particularly adorable) dog, it's well worth considering.

DID YOU KNOW ... ?

- Longevity in domestic dogs depends on the care they receive, their breed, and body size.

- In general, larger breeds have shorter lifespans.

- Many giant dog breeds average only 7 or 8 years, while some small terrier breeds might live as long as 20 years.

- The average lifespan for mixed-breed and midsize dogs is about 13 to 14 years. The longest-lived dog with reliable documentation died at 29 in 1939.

"I used to look at my dog and think, 'If you were a little smarter you could tell me what you were thinking,' and he'd look at me like he was saying, 'If you were a little smarter, I wouldn't have to.'

Fred Jungclaus

Teenage
tearaways!

chapter 3
Teenage tearaways

So, the first month has passed, and everything is going well. Worms, fleas and injections are all sorted, so surely it's plain sailing from here on? Sorry to disappoint, but the next few months are just as crucial as the first, because your puppy is starting to grow up – and we all know that can spell trouble!

Kids come first

For many people, when they think about taking on a new dog, their big fear is that it won't get on with the kids – and maybe it'll even bite them. While this can be a worry, especially if you have a bigger breed dog, here are a few key things to remember which should prevent any problems.

Pack up your troubles …

Firstly, don't forget that dogs are pack animals and your family is their new pack. A happy, well-behaved dog knows his place – and that place is at the bottom of the social order (well, perhaps above the cat!) If you have kids, it's essential that the dog knows that the kids are above him in the pack – otherwise he might try and exert dominance over them and that's when problems can occur.

House rules

Lay down some clear house rules from day one which make it clear that the kids have more rights than the dog. For example, keep the dog downstairs and off the sofa, and make sure he doesn't get his dinner until after you and the kids have had yours. If you stick to these rules, you should never have any problems with an over-dominant dog in the family.

That's mine!

The second tip to stop your dog from causing trouble with the kids is to put all of her toys in a box which the kids control. When they want to play with her, they get the box out and give the dog a toy to play with. At the end of the game, the kids pick up the toys and put them back in the box. This way, the dog knows that the kids are above her in the pack pecking order because they control the toys.

Quick tip

WAIT!

The last tip for dealing with a teenage dog that's getting above his station is to use a bit of door discipline. What this means is that everyone in the family from the baby to granny should always go through doors before the dog. Make him wait, especially when you're going out of the front or back door. He should sit obediently until you've opened the door, walked through, and called him.

"The greatest pleasure of a dog is that you may make a fool of yourself with him, and not only will he not scold you, but he will make a fool of himself, too.

Samuel Butler

Planes, trains and ... skateboards!

The world can be a confusing place for a young dog, and so it's not surprising that they can get very upset by some of the stranger things we expect them to cope with.

Take cars for example. They might seem very normal and mundane to us, but to a dog that has never seen the world move in front of his eyes like that, they can be very scary indeed! And a scared dog, barking and growling at the steering wheel, is no fun for anyone.

The best tip for avoiding these kinds of problems is to introduce your dog at an early stage to anything likely to cause fear so he can get used to it while his mind is still open to new ideas. This window of opportunity generally lasts until they are about four months old – so as soon as your dog is fully protected with his vaccinations, get him out and about meeting and greeting!

Things to get your dog used to ...

- Going in the car
- Meeting people in wheelchairs
- People on bicycles
- Kids on skateboards
- The window cleaner
- The dustbin men
- The postman
- Shopping trolleys
- Cats
- Farm animals

And last but not least, don't forget ... men with beards!
(A surprising number of unsocialised dogs will bark and growl at a bearded man and it can get a little embarrassing!)

Built to go the extra mile

Most dogs, it seems, are born to run. They can run for long periods of time and over long distances. What makes them so well adapted for running? Lots of things!

As a dog runs, its body works like a bellows. A galloping dog takes one breath with each stride. When its back extends, it's easy for the lungs to expand and the dog inhales. When its back flexes, the lungs are compressed, squeezing out air, and the dog exhales.

The long, lean legs of many dogs make running a breeze because it takes relatively little energy to pump them back and forth. Dogs with the longest legs relative to their body size are usually the fastest runners because they take the longest strides. Dogs with shorter, squat legs are usually not very fast runners.

Hard-working muscles need lots of oxygen. Without that extra oxygen, muscles tire and begin to ache, causing both dogs and us to slow down. When dogs run, their heart rate skyrockets, pumping oxygen-rich blood to the muscles. In fact, a snoozing dog has a heart rate about the same as a resting human, 80 beats per minute. A working dog's heart rate can reach 274 beats a minute, almost double the rate of a healthy, active human. No wonder dogs can keep going after most people are exhausted!

It's dog-eat-dog out there!

There's nothing worse than a dog that launches into a mad frenzy of barking and biting whenever he sees another dog. It ruins those quiet country strolls, not to mention the potential for a really nasty bite for any poor dog who gets attacked (or any person who gets caught in the crossfire).

So how do you prevent your dog from being aggressive to other dogs? Well my next tip should make sure your puppy turns into a pacifist pooch not a dangerous dog.

Party time!

To avoid doggy aggression, the thing to do is get your puppy used to other dogs at an early stage. Much like socialising him with cars and bicycles, you've got to get him used to interacting with other dogs when he's young enough to learn the lesson. And the best way to do this is to go to a puppy party.

Now you might be wondering what on earth a puppy party is – and if you were expecting music and dancing dachshunds then you're in for a disappointment! Puppy parties are in fact all about new puppies meeting each other and getting the hang of all those vital social skills that are key to avoiding trouble when they're older. They usually take place at vets or puppy training schools, and any puppies that have had their first vaccinations are welcomed along. As well as meeting lots of other puppies, these parties are also an opportunity for new 'parents' to learn more about training and general health issues.

DON'T FORGET THE OLD BOY

If you've got an older dog in the family and you bring along a new pup, the old dog can have his nose put out of joint by all the attention and fuss the new puppy is getting. Make sure you don't forget to give the old boy lots of walks and cuddles, as this will reassure him that the new whippersnapper hasn't entirely taken over the family.

Beware the young pretender

Another thing to watch out for, if you already have a dog when you bring along a puppy, is trouble between the two of them. In time, the puppy might well become the dominant dog in the family, but until she is old enough and confident enough to take on the older dog's crown, you should make sure you reinforce the older dog's position as top dog. Feed him first and give him pats and cuddles before you give attention to the puppy. This way she will know her place and be less likely to cause trouble, and the old boy will be reassured and not feel the need to be aggressive to the pup.

DID YOU KNOW ... ?

A dog bite is less likely to cause infection than a human bite, although most humans don't need to be quarantined for rabies!

You're collared!

Now pup is old enough to be heading out into the great outside world for walks, it's time to equip him with a suitable lead and collar. Being able to safely and effectively restrain your dog is essential, especially when you're walking him on roads.

There are hundreds of different styles and sizes to choose from but here are a few key things to remember:

- A collar will be on your dog all the time, so make sure it is well-made and comfortable.

- Never use choke chains as these can be very dangerous and painful.

- Dogs with thin and delicate necks, such as greyhounds, lurchers and whippets should have extra wide collars so they don't dig in and cause damage.

- Extendable leads are great for young dogs as they can have a good run around without disappearing into the distance.

- Head collars are great for strong dogs and those who don't get on with other dogs, because you have much more control, and can turn their heads away from other dogs. This breaks their eye-contact, and greatly reduces the likelihood of aggressive behaviour.

- Body harnesses are also really good, especially for strong little dogs such as terriers, which tend to pull on the lead a lot. The harness spreads the load out across the chest, which is more comfortable for the dog, and gives you more control.

- Always take a collar off if you are leaving her in a crate for any length of time on her own because it can get caught on the bars.

And of course there's just one more thing to remember – she's got to look good, so pick a lead and collar which suits her colouring and breed!

"You can say any foolish thing to a dog, and the dog will give you a look that says, 'My God, you're right! I never would have thought of that!"

Dave Berry

Baby blues

If you're brave enough to have taken on a new puppy at the same time as having a baby, then there are a few extra things to remember. Firstly never leave the dog and baby alone together – you can never predict a dog's behaviour 100% and it's not worth taking any risks. Secondly, make sure that the dog gets used to the baby as soon as possible (under supervision of course) – and also gets used to the fact that the baby is well above him in the pack order. And finally, take extra care with hygiene as dogs can pose a health risk to babies and young children via roundworm eggs and bacteria in their faeces.

A little place of her own

Giving pup a place of her own in the form of a puppy crate is a modern idea which can work really well for juvenile dogs. The crates are basically large cages, and they work by giving the pup somewhere of her own to spend time, and help to train and discipline her. If you want to use a crate, make sure you buy a big enough one for your dog, and line it with a comfy bed. Encourage her to spend time in there every day, but leave the door open as much as you can. It's also a good idea to feed her in the crate and occasionally put a treat in there so she associates being in there with good things.

The crate shouldn't be used as a 'sin-bin' for hours on end, but they can be very useful for keeping an un-supervised puppy out of mischief, or as somewhere for an over-excited puppy to go to calm down for a while – much like sending a troublesome teenager to their room!

Exercise

One of the best things about owning a dog is the exercise you both get. Two walks a day, come rain or shine, does wonders for both you and your new friend, but there are a few things to be aware of before you go racing off across the hills. Here are a few tips to help you out:

Establish a routine

Having a familiar daily routine is really important for young dogs, so try to get into the habit of walking her at roughly the same time every day. A good walk first thing and then again in the early evening is the minimum any dog should get – but ideally take her out for three walks if you have the time.

Quick tip

IT'S WORTH THE WAIT
Never take your dog out in public areas or parks until a week after their second puppy vaccination. Diseases like distemper and parvovirus are still around, and unvaccinated dogs can pick them up from other dogs, and even foxes.

Lead the way

To begin with, always keep your puppy on the lead. An overexcited puppy can easily disappear into the undergrowth and not be seen for hours, so it's best to keep him under control until he's got used to the park and you've done some basic training.

Avoid the crowds

When you first start taking your dog out in parks and woods, try to avoid the busy times when there are loads of dogs and people about. This will help your dog get used to all the interesting smells and sights of the countryside, without the added excitement of lots of other dogs.

Don't overdo it!

One of the biggest mistakes people make with young dogs is over-exercising them. Overdoing energetic walks—especially when the dog is doing lots of running—can cause serious health problems later in life. The main problem is joint disease (arthritis), and this is particularly serious in larger dogs. If they do too much running and jumping when their joints are still developing (up to two years of age for really big dogs), the cartilage can be damaged and this can leave them with permanent problems including severe lameness.

Some experts recommend that big dogs should have no off-lead exercise at all until they are two years old, but most vets advise a slightly less strict regime. The key tip is to take your dog for lots of short walks, mainly on the lead, rather than going out for long periods in one go.

"Dogs feel very strongly that they should always go with you in the car, in case the need should arise for them to bark violently at nothing right in your ear."

Dave Barr

Dogs behaving badly!

chapter 4
Dogs behaving badly

Having a badly behaved dog can be a real nightmare. Whether he barks all night, bites the postman or just leaps up at strangers with muddy paws, owning a dog with behavioural problems can make your life a real misery if you're not careful.

So how do you prevent your dog becoming a hound from hell? Well it's all in his training, and here are a few top tips to help you make sure your dog learns impeccable manners!

It's never too early to start

Teaching your dog good behaviour should start as soon as you get her home. Puppies are far more receptive to new ideas than older dogs, and while it's not true that you can't teach an old dog new tricks, it certainly does get harder to train dogs as they mature.

Start with a few really simple things, like basic discipline using positive rewards for good behaviour. If you give your puppy a nice treat whenever she does something right such as wee outside, or get off the sofa when she's told to, she'll quickly realise that good behaviour leads to nice things happening, and this will make it far easier to train her properly later on.

It pays to be nice

Lots of people think that the only way to train a dog is to shout at him loudly and give him a smack whenever he does something wrong. This is entirely wrong, and negative training such like this should be used as sparingly as possible – and physical discipline should never be required.

It's much more effective to reward the dog whenever he does the right thing, as this motivates the dog to follow your commands and not to misbehave.

Negative commands should only be used when a dog is doing something he really knows he shouldn't be – such as trying to steal a sly sausage off the kitchen table!

Quick tip

PAY ATTENTION!

Attention is everything for a puppy – it's what they crave, and by giving it to them or denying them, you can easily teach them what you want them to do. For example, puppies which keep playfully biting can be a real pain, and it's important to let them know that it's not acceptable behaviour. Do this by stopping any games you are playing as soon as they get too frisky. Simply walk away with a minimum of fuss and come back a few minutes later when they've settled down. If they start to nip again, just get up and go. They will very quickly learn that they have to be good if they want attention.

"If you think dogs can't count, try putting three dog biscuits in your pocket and then giving Fido only two of them.

Phil Pastoret

Make it click!

One of the best innovations in dog training has been the clicker. These are small plastic devices which make a loud 'click' when you press them. Now you might be wondering how a click can help train a dog – well the answer is in those famous Pavlovian dogs that learnt to salivate whenever they heard a bell. It happened because they were always fed whenever a bell sounded, and so they quickly began to associate the sound of the bell with eating. Later on, they still subconsciously associated the sound of a bell with food, and so they produced saliva, even though there wasn't food around anymore when the bell rang.

It is really easy to use this principle in dog training. All you do is get your dog to associate the sound of the clicker with a reward, such as a biscuit. Whenever he does something good, like sit on command, you click the clicker and give him a treat. After a while, you can start to leave out the treats and just click the clicker, as you dog will have come to associate the sound of the click with a reward – in effect the click itself has become the reward in the dog's mind.

Sausages!

Here's a tip for you if you're having trouble getting your dog to respond to rewards out in the park. Try a bit of garlic sausage because this is really strong smelling and will get the dog's attention much more effectively than less pungent treats. Edam cheese is another favourite with lots of dogs and the smell will usually make them sit and take notice!

Titbits and treats

Rewarding your dog for good behaviour is an essential part of the training process and one of the easiest and most effective ways of rewarding a dog is by giving him a little bit of food. There are lots of processed treats available, but these are not always the healthiest option, especially if you're doing lots of training and giving the dog many treats. Instead of using these manufactured treats why not consider something a bit more healthy such as a small piece of freshly cooked meat (chicken and liver are real favourites) or even a piece of fruit or veg. It's also a good idea to vary the treats as this will keep your dog's enthusiasm up and also make his diet more varied and healthy.

Come back ... please!

If there's one command you really want to work with your dog, it's 'here!'. There is nothing worse than spending hours searching for your dog when he's disappeared in the park after completely ignoring your desperate shouts, not to mention the dangers of him running onto a road, or chasing other dogs, or people.

Getting your dog to come back on command requires a bit of effort, but if you remember a few important tips, you should have him bounding back to you within a few days.

Sing when you're winning

Firstly, and most importantly, always make sure that when you begin teaching him to come back, you only ever give the command 'here!' or 'come!' when he is actually coming back to you anyway. If you shout at him to come back when he's racing away in the opposite direction with his attention focused on a rabbit or ball, he'll ignore you – and worse than that, he won't associate the command with the action of going back to you. So wait until he's racing back towards you and then shout the command out – that way he'll quickly associate the command with running back to you and will learn to come back whenever you call – well most of the time anyway!

Sit!

This is one of the basic commands your dog should obey – and also one of the easiest to teach. A good tip for getting your dog to sit really easily is to take a small treat and hold it above his nose, and then move the treat slightly backwards. As his eyes follow the treat, his back end will naturally drop down towards the ground. As this happens, give him the 'Sit!' command so he associates the action with the word. Once his bottom is down, give him lots of praise and let him eat the treat (and give the clicker a click if you are using that method). Easy!

Down boy!

A dog that is constantly jumping up at people can be a real problem – and be a nightmare for you the owner, and for anyone who comes too close on a muddy day (they always seem to jump up at people when they've just walked through a particularly muddy puddle, and choose the people wearing the most expensive clothes!).

But don't despair if you've got a jumping Jack Russell or a pawing Papillion, here's a simple tip to help you cure this problem. The thing to do is to ask anyone who has regular contact with her to stick to the following rule: whenever she jumps up, fold your arms and turn your back on her so she falls back down. Then, ask her to sit, and only give her the attention she wants when she's calmly sitting down.

Get as many people as possible to stick to this rule, and she'll soon realise that the best way to get attention is to stay with all four feet on the ground, and not to leap up at people.

DID YOU KNOW ... ?
A dog's ear is very sensitive, full of sensory nerves that help to preserve hearing. Never blow into a dog's ear, even gently this can hurt a dog. It's not the actual act of wind, but the frequency at which you blow. It's like running your fingernails down a blackboard, amplified hundreds of times.

Grit those teeth

You're out in the park and everything is going well. Fred is obeying all your commands and behaving impeccably ... just as you are about to head home he suddenly spots a rabbit in the hedge and he's off. You shout yourself hoarse but to no avail – he's gone and there's no sign of him for ages, leaving you fuming impatiently, lead in hand.

Then he suddenly reappears and comes bounding back, tail wagging as if nothing has happened. You are furious though, and give him a piece of your mind for keeping you waiting for so long. He hangs his head in shame and looks thoroughly dejected.

Now you might well think that this was the right thing to do. After all, he's been told off for running away, and looks like he's learnt his lesson. However that's not quite how Fred will have seen things. In his mind, he was having a great time chasing the rabbit, and then when he finally decided to obey your command and go back to you, what did he get for his trouble – a great big telling off! So here's what you should do ...

In these situations just grit your teeth and make yourself praise him for coming back to you. Forget the fact that he's been disobeying you for hours, and concentrate on reinforcing his good behaviour. It might be hard to do, but if you tell him off, he'll only think that he's in trouble for coming back to you, and that's not going to encourage him to come back again.

Calm down dear – it's only the doorbell!

Many dogs get really overexcited whenever the door bell goes, leaping up in a whirlwind of barking and jumping. This can be a bit off-putting for any visitors to the house, not to mention driving you up the wall.

Here are two good tips for dealing with this kind of behavioural problem:

- **Number One**
  Get her used to the doorbell by ringing it regularly throughout the day and opening the door to show that nothing exciting is out there.

- **Number Two**
  If she still gets overexcited at the sound of the bell, take her off into the kitchen (or her crate if you have one) for a few minutes of quiet time every time the bell goes. Only let her out to meet the visitor once she's totally calmed down.

What have you done to the house?!

One of the most common problems which drive people and their hounds to pet behaviourists is separation anxiety. This commonly manifests itself as destructive behaviour, such as chewing the furniture, or loud, constant barking whenever the dog is left alone.

This can be a really tricky problem to sort out, but if you catch it early, these tips should help:

Home alone

Get him used to you leaving the house in small stages.
First, just pick up your keys and walk towards the door. Do this
a few times throughout the day without actually going out and
totally ignore the dog even if he barks. After a while, he should
get used to this, and you can go a stage further by opening
and closing the front door. Finally, leave the house for short
periods at a time, making sure you totally ignore any bad
behaviour. When you come back in, wait until he's completely
calmed down before giving him any attention.

His master's voice

If you're still not getting anywhere, try making a tape or CD
with your voice on it – read a book or just talk away, the
content doesn't matter. Play the recording on the stereo in the
living room and put the dog in the kitchen. This way he'll be
tricked into thinking you're still at home when you're out!

Quick tip

TAKE IT EASY ...
Finally, when you do come back from being out of the
house, the worst thing you can do is to make a big fuss
of the dog. This only serves to reinforce the drama of you
leaving and coming back in the dog's mind, so it's much
better to wait until he's really settled down before giving
him any attention. This way he'll start to realise that you
going out is not such a big deal after all, and he doesn't
have to get so wound up by it.

If you need help …

Here are my top six places to look for help if your dog's behaviour is not top of the class!

1. **Your vet**
   Most modern vets know a lot about behaviour and should be the first place you go for help.

2. **The bookshop**
   There are literally hundreds of books on dog behaviour available, and a good one will be invaluable if your dog is causing trouble.

3. **The Association of Pet Dog Trainers**
   Set up in 1995, this organisation helps people find top quality dog trainers. Their website is **www.apdt.co.uk.**

4. **The Kennel Club**
   As well as looking after pedigree dogs and shows, the Kennel Club also run schemes to promote good dog behaviour and socialisation. Their U.K. number is 0870 606 6750 and their website is **www.the-kennel-club.org.uk**.

5. **The Association of Pet Behaviour Counsellors**
   A great place to help you find a behaviour specialist. Check out their website at **www.spbc.org.uk.**

6. **Internet dog forums**
   There are many of these chat rooms all over the world and dog owners love to share information about their pets. You might just find someone with the same breed and the same problem and get some good advice to help you with the behaviour issue.

Dogs understand your moods and your thoughts, and if you are thinking unpleasant things about your dog, he will pick it up and be downhearted.

Barbara Woodhouse

Nose to tail health

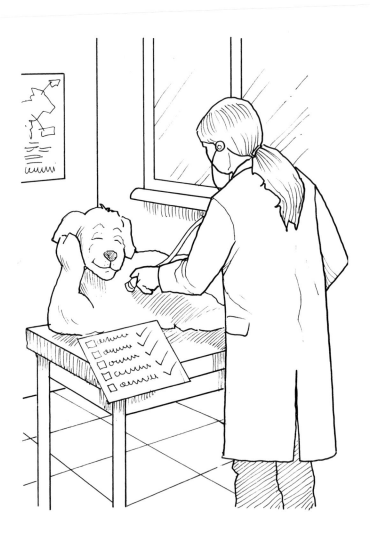

chapter 5
Nose to tail health

Keeping your beloved dog in good health can be hard work, but if you pay attention to these tips, your dog should stay in the peak of health for many years to come.

Grooming can be fun ... honest!

For some dogs, grooming can be a really unpleasant experience. They're poked, prodded, brushed, clipped and even bathed, when they'd much rather be lazing in front of the fire or chasing a squirrel. However, grooming doesn't have to be like this. If you follow a few basic principles early on, dogs can learn to love grooming, and this will make looking after them a whole lot easier.

The key to fun grooming is to associate all the stages of grooming, such as handling, stroking, brushing and clipping, with positive rewards such as treats. Start by gently rubbing your dog's coat, and give her a treat as you are doing this. Keep repeating this until your dog shows signs of looking forward to being stroked. Then simply repeat this for brushing, clipping, and even bathing, and your dog will soon learn that all these things bring rewards. Within a few weeks she'll be rolling over enthusiastically as soon as you reach for the brush!

A brush a day keeps the vet away!

Grooming is not only vital for keeping your dog's coat in tiptop condition, it is also an excellent way of checking your dog over from nose to tail on a regular basis. Anything unusual, such as a lump, swelling or patch of sore skin will be easily spotted and enable you to get some veterinary advice as soon as possible.

Most dogs need occasional grooming – perhaps a good brush once a week and the odd trip to a grooming parlour for a clip and bath – but some breeds need far more coat care. Long haired breeds such as Afghan Hounds require daily attention to their coats, and it's well worth asking an experienced groomer for advice with these specialised breeds.

Quick tip

PLAYTIME!

Playing with your dog is an excellent way of making sure you are really in tune with his body and helps you spot any potential problems early. A bit of hands-on rough and tumble will ensure you are familiar with everything about him, from the texture of his coat, to the length of his nails. Try to run your hands over as much of his body as you can during your playtime sessions, as this is the best way of finding lumps and bumps before they are big enough to see from a distance.

Grass seeds – the hidden enemy …

What would you guess to be the biggest threat to dogs walking in fields of grass? Perhaps a snake bite or a sting from a bee, or even the thorn of a bramble in the hedgerow? Well, it's none of the above. The culprits are tiny grass seeds that come out in the mid to late summer. These innocent-looking awns can be really nasty, because they get trapped in the fur of dogs' ears and feet, and once there, they can burrow into the skin, and cause horrible infections.

When a grass awn blows off the stalk and settles on the ground, it immediately starts germinating and working its way down into the soil. Unfortunately, warm, moist doggy skin provides much the same environment! Grass awns can easily stick to your pet's coat as it wanders through the grass. Long-haired and long-eared dogs are most susceptible to this problem, but all breeds can be affected.

The reason they're so unpleasant is their barbed shape. This means that once they've pierced the skin, they can only move in one direction – deeper into your pet's flesh. As the dog moves, the seed will gradually work its way in to the foot or ear, and cause a painful swelling filled with infection.

Often the first a dog owner will know is when the dog goes lame and is constantly licking his foot, or his ear develops a foul smell. Attempts to remove the awn without veterinary assistance are futile. In addition to becoming imbedded in the skin, the prickly seeds can become tangled in your pet's coat, causing severe matting making them almost impossible to brush or comb out.

... the solution

There is a way of preventing grass seed problems though, and that is to check your dog's ears and feet thoroughly after every walk in grassy areas in summer. Make a habit of grooming your dog after each walk, to keep his coat clean and matt-free, and to check for grass awns or other irritating debris. It's mainly spaniels and terriers which suffer from this problem, but any dog with hairy ears or feet should be checked. It's well worth the effort, as it could save your dog from a very nasty infection – and you from a big vet bill!

Nails

There's a common misconception amongst many dog owners that all dogs need their nails clipped on a regular basis. In fact, most active dogs that walk at least some of the time on hard surfaces like roads, generally never need their nails doing. It's usually older dogs or those who exercise solely on grass who need the occasional trim, but here's a tip that will help you decide whether your dog's nails need attention – and it's all to do with letters ...

A nail of the perfect length should look like a slightly long letter 'r' (where the end of the pad is the straight stem of the letter, and curved top represents the nail). Nails which are overgrown start to look more like a letter 'p', as the nail grows round and heads back towards the pad. The correct length is when the nail forms a quarter circle when viewed from the side —any longer than this, and you should give the nails a trim— or pop down to your vet for a quick pedicure!

Half of the battle of nail clipping can be won by choosing the right nail clippers for your dog. Cheap, flimsy clippers can make the whole job much more difficult and uncomfortable for the dog, and are usually a false economy. Invest in a good, solid pair of clippers, and buy ones which are suitable for the size of your dog. The most effective clippers are those which encircle the nail and act like a guillotine. Clippers which are open ended tend to squeeze the nail painfully before they cut, and should be avoided.

Don't make a drama out of a crisis!

Lots of dogs hate having their nails clipped and even just the sight of the clippers can send them into an anxious frenzy!

The best way to avoid this kind of drama at nail-trimming time is to get the dog accustomed to the clippers gradually over several weeks. It helps if you can do this when she is as young as possible, but older dogs can also be helped to overcome a fear of nail clipping using the same principle.

All you need to do is get her to associate everything about nail clipping with good things. So start by playing with her feet and giving her a treat. Then gradually bring the clippers in and have them in you hands as you touch her feet (but don't clip yet), again giving her treats as you do so. Then finally, after a few weeks of repeating this several times a day, gently start trimming the very ends of her nails and giving her a treat as you do so.

Follow this advice, and your dog should never have a problem with having her nails trimmed.

"One reason
a dog can be such
a comfort when
you're feeling blue
is that he doesn't
try to find out why.

Anon

Watch that quick!

The quick is the red part of the nail which is full of nerves and blood vessels, and you must be really careful not to cut this when you are trimming a dog's nails. If you do, it is really painful for the dog, and can cause some quite unpleasant bleeding which can be hard to stop.

The best tip for avoiding this is to identify the quick and make sure you cut the nail at least 3 or 4mm ($^1/_8$") below the end of it. In dogs with light-coloured nails this is usually pretty easy as the quick is visible as the red area at the top of the nail. Black nails are much harder, because it is impossible to see the quick. What you should do with these nails is line the clippers up with the bottom of the pad, and check that your cut will leave a full quarter circle of nail when you look side on. If in doubt, leave an extra few millimetres – it's not worth taking the risk of hitting the quick.

Doggy breath

Having a big slobbery kiss from your dog can be a lovely sign of affection – but if his mouth is full of rotten teeth the experience can be a whole lot less enjoyable! And of course there are more serious consequences of your dog having bad teeth. Dental problems can be very painful, put your dog off his food, and even cause infections to spread to other parts of the body via the bloodstream. So keeping those doggy gnashers in tiptop condition will do more than just make those doggy kisses bearable – it will help to keep your dog in good health from nose to tail. Here are my top teeth tips for your dog:

Brush up

We all brush our teeth everyday, but how many people think about doing the same for their dog? However, just imagine what your teeth would be like in a few years' time if you never brushed them – pretty unpleasant! In fact not brushing is one of the big reasons why so many dogs have rotten teeth. Food and bacteria collect on the teeth, leading to tartar build up and dental decay.

Brushing your dog's teeth is not very hard, and it's well worth getting into a regular routine where you give his teeth a good cleaning every day. You must use a special soft doggy toothbrush and toothpaste made for dogs. There are lots of lovely flavours available, like beef and chicken, and they are formulated so as to be safe for the dog to swallow (as it's hard to ask a dog to rinse and spit!)

As with all new things, get your dog used to having his teeth brushed gradually, using lots of treats and rewards for good behaviour. Brush using a circular motion with the tip of the brush at 45 degrees to the teeth, and work your way around all of his teeth.

Wild bones

You might wonder what happens to all the wild dogs, wolves and foxes which have survived quite happily for thousands of years without so much as a whiff of toothpaste – do they all have horrible teeth, or could it be they've got a different way of keeping their teeth clean?

The answer lies in the diet of these wild canines. They're all scavengers and spend a lot of time chewing over the carcasses of other animals—and most importantly—grinding their teeth on the bones. This action of gnawing away on hard bones works wonders for their teeth, as it cleans away any food scraps and bacteria, just like brushing does.

A bone a day keeps the dentist away

It's not just wild dogs who can keep their teeth clean by gnawing bones. Domestic dogs love chewing bones and it's a great way of preventing dental problems. I recommend giving all dogs a good bone to chew on at least once a month. Simply pop down to your butcher and ask for a nice meaty bone – and your dog will spend hours happily chewing away, and his teeth will be as clean as a whistle by the time he's finished!

There's just one really important thing to remember about bones though, and that is that the bone must be raw. Cooked bones are dangerous because they splinter and leave sharp fragments.

Quick tip

IT'S GOOD TO MAKE A PIG'S EAR OF SOME THINGS ...
Here's a good tip for dogs who don't like chewing bones. Buy her a dried pig's ear from the pet shop. These are just like the crackling you have with your Sunday roast pork, and are great for cleaning dog's teeth. Just don't give her too many though because they are very salty and fattening, so one or two a month is about right.

'Ear's a few good tips ...

If I had a pound for every dog on the planet who suffered from bad ears, I'd be a rich vet indeed. Ear infections are one of the most common problems affecting dogs, and there are all sorts of causes, from tiny mites to waxy infections. Here are a few tips to help you help your dog and keep his ears fresh and healthy.

Hairy ear monsters

Ever wondered why some dogs get ear problems and some don't? Well the answer usually comes down to the shape of their ear, and the amount of hair there is around the ear opening. Dogs like spaniels which have very hairy ears which flop down by the sides of their head tend to have far more trouble with ear infections than short-haired dogs with pointy ears. This is because the thick fur and floppy ears tend to prevent air circulating in and out of the ear, making them perfect for bacteria to breed in.

Plucked ears are healthy ears

To help prevent ear infections in dogs with hairy ears, the best thing to do is to pluck as much hair as you can out of the ear. Arm yourself with a pair of tweezers and grab hold of the hairs poking out of the ear canal in little clumps — then pull with a swift tug. You should be able to pluck out most of the hair this way, and if you only pull a few hairs at a time, it shouldn't be too uncomfortable for the dog. If he really doesn't like it, you might want to get your groomer or vet to do it for you.

Don't go too deep ...

A dog's ear canal goes straight down before turning a corner and heading in towards his head. At the end of this horizontal part is the delicate ear drum, and you must be really careful not to damage this when you are cleaning your dog's ears. Most problems occur when people use cotton wool buds, because these can reach all the way down to the ear drum.

However there is a way of making sure you never cause any problems, even if you are using buds. The tip is to hold the ear tip up nice and high, and push the cotton bud down parallel to the ear and the side of his head. When it reaches the bottom of the vertical part of the ear canal you will safely hit the corner of the canal not the ear drum. You can be quite vigorous using this method, as there is no way you will hit the ear drum as long as you keep the cotton bud parallel to his head.

At the end of the exercise a bit of fuss and a few treats should be the order of the day!

Wash and wax

If your dog has waxy ears it's important to clean them out effectively or infection is likely to set in. The best thing to use is a proper ear cleaner which you can get from your vet or pet shop.

My top tip for cleaning out a waxy ear is to hold the tip of your dog's ear in one hand and hold it up vertically. This will open the ear canal up, and allow you to pour a generous amount of cleaner down the ear. Then gently massage the ear canal with you other hand to loosen the wax, before wiping it out with a ball of cotton wool.

Joe's healthcare diary

Every day

- Brush teeth.
- A good session of hands-on play, checking all over for any lumps or bumps.
- Check feet and ears for grass seeds after walks in the summer.
- Check eyes for discharges and redness.
- Groom long-haired breeds.

Every week

- Check ears for signs of wax.
- Groom.
- Give dental chew to keep teeth clean.
- Check coat carefully for fleas.

Every month

- Check nails and trim if necessary.
- Check ears and pluck away any overgrowing fur.
- Give big raw bone or pig's ear to chew on.
- Examine teeth and consider a veterinary opinion if in doubt.
- Treat for fleas (exact frequency depends on the product being used).

Every three months

- Worm with a good quality worming tablet.

Every year

- Annual check up and vaccinations at your vet.

Hot dogs ... and cool dogs

Dogs need a way to get rid of excess heat. Whereas humans sweat, dogs pant. An overheated dog breathes in and out through its mouth. With each pant, dogs inhale cool air. As the cool air moves into the lungs, it absorbs heat and moisture. When dogs exhale hot breath across a wet tongue, water evaporates, cooling their bodies. To maximize heat loss, panting dogs direct warm blood to their tongue to be cooled. The hot, moist air the dog exhales is warmer than if it exited the nose, helping to rapidly dump body heat. But just like sweating, panting cools by evaporation and a panting dog needs access to plenty of drinking water.

Unless it's a really hot day, a resting dog doesn't generate excess body heat. A resting dog breathes normally, in and out through its nose. Inhaled air is warmed and moistened by passing through the nose on its way to the lungs. On the reverse trip, exhaled air returns some of its warmth and water to the body as it flows through the previously cooled nose. Breathing in and out through the nose preserves body fluids and heat, keeping the dog hydrated.

Dogs that are only slightly hot will breathe in the nose and out the mouth. To breathe in one way and out another, dogs use their tongues to direct air-flow. When the tongue moves back the dog inhales through the nose. As it moves forward, air moves out through the mouth. All of this happening at least 5 times a second!

I've seen a look
in dogs' eyes,
a quickly vanishing
look of amazed
contempt, and
I am convinced that
basically dogs think
humans are nuts.

John Steinbeck

Food, glorious food!

chapter 6

chapter 6
Food, glorious food!

There's a well-known saying "you are what you eat", and this applies just as much to your dog as to yourself. Get your dog's food wrong and he could end up with some serious health problems, so it's well worth making sure your dog has a healthy diet which suits his individual requirements. Here are some healthy eating tips to keep your dog fit and full!

Remember the ancestors

When thinking about the food your dog eats, it's well worth bearing in mind the fact that all modern domestic dogs are descended from wolves and wild dogs. These ancient animals were omnivorous scavengers – in other words they ate anything and everything they could get their teeth into! The main part of their diet would have been the remains of carcasses left behind by predators, and so bones, meat, and vegetable matter from the animal's stomach would have all been chewed up by these scavenging canines.

Now I'm not for a moment suggesting that you try and feed your pet dog on anything like this kind of diet, but it is important that all the key ingredients and nutrients from this wild diet are present in your modern dog's dinner. Your dog needs this mix of vegetable matter and meat in order to stay healthy, and there are several different of ways to achieve this kind of balanced diet.

A complete dog's dinner

The easiest way of feeding your dog the right mix of nutrients is to give her one of the complete foods available. These are either available as wet foods, in tins or pouches, or as dried kibbles. Each chunk of the wet food, or biscuit of the dried diets, is specially formulated to contain all the protein, fat, carbohydrate, vitamins and minerals your dog needs.

Cheap as ... chicken feathers!

As with most things in life, you really get what you pay for with complete dog foods. It's all very well saving money by buying the cheapest food from the supermarket, but just remember that the reason it costs so little is that it's made from the very cheapest ingredients. This can include such delicacies as feathers, feet and other animal by-products, and usually very little real meat. While foods like this will generally contain all the basic nutrients your dog needs, they will also contain a lot of artificial preservatives, flavours and colours (in order to disguise the taste of all those chicken feet and feathers!). They are not good for the long term health of your dog, and are best avoided if at all possible.

> **DID YOU KNOW ... ?**
> Dogs have far fewer taste buds than people – they have about 1,700 on their tongues, while we humans have about 9,000 – and it is the smell that initially attracts them to a particular food.

A meal fit for a dog

At the other end of the dog food spectrum are premium and super-premium complete diets. These are a lot more expensive than the cheaper brands, but are much better for your dog. The best brands don't use artificial chemicals or animal by-products, just real meat protein and a healthy carbohydrate source such as brown rice. If your budget will stretch to one of these top brands, it's well worth the extra, as your dog is much more likely to live a happier and healthier life as a result.

Wet or dry?

Variety is the spice of life and I think dogs appreciate a little variation and excitement in their food. Dried biscuits are generally considered to be the most healthy option for everyday feeding (because they help keep the teeth clean), but day in, day out these diets can get a little dull, however tasty the food. Why not mix in some pouches of meaty chunks every few days to give the meal a little extra texture and taste.

Fresh is best

Even better than mixing pouches of meaty chunks into your dog's dried food, why not go one step further and cook him up some fresh food every now and then? Cooking for your dog everyday is not practical for most people – and isn't generally recommended unless you are very knowledgeable about nutrition, as it's easy to cause problems if you don't feed a well-balanced diet. However, a weekly meal of fresh meat and veg is a great way of treating your dog and giving him some really healthy, fresh food in his diet.

Top five recipes for home-cooked doggie dinners …

(Don't forget to serve them cold!)

1. **Chicken**
   Chicken breast, roast or boiled, covered in a puree of carrot, courgette and sweet potato.

2. **Steak**
   Chunks of braising steak boiled up with vegetables and poured over some well-cooked brown rice.

3. **Offal**
   Liver and kidney casserole – cook some fresh pieces of liver and kidney together with assorted veg (avoid onion) and some stock to make a lovely, healthy dish full of vitamins and minerals.

4. **Boiled eggs**
   On their own or mixed in with some meat and veg, soft-boiled eggs are a great source of healthy protein.

5. **Fido's fruit smoothie!**
   Lots of dogs love fresh fruit – and it's really good for them as well. Just mix up any ripe fruit you have, blend them together, and serve – a glass for you, and a bowlful for Fido!

For more great doggie dinners check out the Healthy recipes for your dog section on page 132 or treat yourself to *The Greatest Doggie Dinners in the World* (ISBN 1-905151-51-6).

Titbits are trouble

You might think it's a bit strange to say that titbits are bad for your dog when I've just suggested cooking up some fresh food for him. Well, titbits are not necessarily bad news, it's just that the titbits most people give their dogs are not usually the healthiest bit of their dinner. It tends to be the fatty scraps of meat which make it into the dog's bowl, and while this is fine in small amounts, giving too much of this kind of high fat food will be bad for your dog and tend to make him overweight. If you like giving the dog some titbits from your plate, try to give him a mix of bits, including some meat and vegetables, and avoid too much fat.

DID YOU KNOW ... ?
That some foods we eat can be poisonous to dogs. Chocolate contains a substance called theobromine which is related to caffeine. Some dogs will react badly to this and show symptoms such as a raised heart rate, vomiting and diarrhoea. It's best to avoid giving chocolate to any dogs just in case, but don't worry too much if your dog eats a small amount – the average 20kg (44lb) dog needs to eat over a kilo of milk chocolate to absorb a dangerous amount of the toxin. Other foods to avoid include onions, mushrooms and grapes as these can all cause problems.

TWICE IS NICE!

Lots of people only feed their dogs once a day, but my tip is to give them two meals a day. Food is such an important thing in most dogs' lives that making them wait a whole day between feeds seems a little bit unfair. Instead, give them half of their daily ration in the morning and half early in the evening. This way they have two meals to look forward to every day which keeps them more contented – and it's better for their digestion.

Keep those vampires away!

Garlic is a real wonder food – and it really can keep blood-sucking vampires away. I'm not talking about Dracula and his evil creatures of the night of course – I'm referring to fleas. These tiny insects do drink the blood of your dog (and you if they get a chance), but just like the mystical vampires, a clove of garlic a day can keep them at bay. Just crush a clove of fresh garlic into his food once a day, and you should find you don't need to use insecticidal sprays or drops as often (it makes him taste terrible to fleas) – and you can sleep easy in the knowledge that should Count Dracula pay a visit, your dog is safe.

Keep it cooked

Some people recommend that dogs should be fed on a diet of raw meat and bones, but whilst this sounds like a very good idea in principle, my tip is to stick to properly cooked food. The main reason is food hygiene. Whilst dogs do have very sturdy digestive systems, and can cope with far more unpleasant bacteria in their food than we can, there still exists a risk that raw food will cause problems, either through bacteria such as salmonella, or parasites such as tapeworm cysts. And there's also a risk to human health if raw meat is being prepared and fed in the kitchen.

Cooking meat protects your dog from these risks, and also aids the digestibility of the food and reduces the fat content. It does have some negative effects, such as reducing the levels of some nutrients, but this will not be in any way significant if your dog is being fed primarily on a complete food.

The main exception is raw bones. Chewing on uncooked bones is great for your dog's overall health as they keep his teeth clean as well as providing loads of minerals to keep his bones strong. Never feed cooked bones, as these can splinter and cause nasty internal problems.

DID YOU KNOW ... ?
Using their swivelling ears like radar dishes, experiments have shown that dogs can locate the source of a sound in 6/100ths of a second.

Stop trouble brewing ...

You've probably always thought that beer was good for you in some way – well that may not be entirely true, but this next tip involving one of the key ingredients of a good pint, certainly is!

Brewer's yeast is an excellent source of many nutrients, especially the B vitamins. Half a teaspoon a day in your dog's food will provide all the B vitamins he needs, as well as important minerals. If you're feeding a top quality food, it should contain brewer's yeast so you don't need to add extra – check the ingredients to make sure.

DID YOU KNOW ... ?

One good way to find out if your dog is getting the proper nutrition is to read the pet food labels. Your dog should be eating a proper well balanced diet including the following:

CARBOHYDRATES: This helps your dog's energy levels, prevents constipation, and includes well-cooked grains, starches, and sugars.

PROTEINS: This is for proper growth and the maintenance and repair of tissues. Protein sources include meat, eggs, fish, and soy products.

FATS: This gives your dog energy, a healthy and shiny coat, and adds flavor to his meal.

VITAMINS AND MINERALS: They are the basis for the day-to-day functioning of your dog and promote good eyesight and growth. Your dog can get vitamins from products like meat, eggs, fish, and vegetables.

Seaweed … ?

Believe it or not, seaweed is an excellent source of all sorts of nutrients, including iodine which is vital for a healthy thyroid gland (to keep the body's metabolism ticking over). And you can get seaweed in tablets (called kelp tablets), so you don't even need to worry about dragging bags of smelly weed home from the beach after your summer holidays! You can get the tablets from a health food shop, and one a day for a medium sized dog 20kg (44lb) will make sure he gets plenty of iodine and salts. Don't overdo the seaweed though, as too much can damage the thyroid gland – check with your vet if you are worried.

Change foods gradually

Here's a tip to help you avoid an upset tummy if you change your dog's diet – make the change to the new food gradually over at least three days. On the first day, feed her three-quarters of her normal diet, mixed in with one quarter of the new food. Then the next day, give her half and half, and on day three, feed her three-quarters new and just a quarter of the original diet. Finally, on day four, she should be ready to eat nothing but the new food.

The reason for making changes like this is to give her digestive system time to adjust to the new food. If you change things too quickly, the bacteria and enzymes aren't suited to the new food, and diarrhoea is a common result.

"He is your friend,
your partner, your
defender, your dog.
You are his life,
his love, his leader.
He will be yours,
faithful and true,
to the last beat
of his heart."

Anon

Weight watchers!

Obesity is a growing problem in dogs (excuse the pun!) with more and more dogs ending up seriously overweight. This can lead to all sorts of health problems, from diabetes and liver disease to arthritis and lameness, and is a major factor in reducing life expectancy in these dogs. So how do you keep your dog's waistline under control? Well here are a few tips to try to keep your dog fighting fit, not fighting the flab!

Healthy eating

As with humans, too much junk food is a recipe for obesity. Cheap processed dog foods tend to be high in fat and low in healthy nutrients. It's much better to spend money on a premium food which will have a healthier balance of ingredients. It might cost more in the short term, but long term the benefits of keeping your dog trim and healthy will save you money on vet bills.

Quick tip

CONTROL THOSE CALORIES

If your dog is overweight, there is one simple way of getting those pounds off him; reduce the amount of calories you are feeding him. There are two easy ways of doing this; either reduce the amount of food you are feeding him, or change his food to a lower calorie diet. There are lots of low calorie dog foods around and these can be really useful in battling the doggy bulge!

Grated veg makes a great filler

If you reduce your dog's rations only to find him looking mournfully up at you begging for more food at the end of each meal, here's an idea to help fill him up without piling on the calories. Simply grate up some raw vegetables such as carrots, parsnip, sweet potato or any green veg and add them to his food. You can add plenty of these grated veg to his food without giving him too many extra calories; and it provides a healthy source of vitamins as well.

Pound off those pounds!

The other key to keeping weight off you dog is, of course, exercise. All those calories that come in from food need to be burnt off through physical exercise, otherwise they will end up turning into fat. Make sure you walk your dog at least twice a day—more if you have time—and try to make the walks as energetic as possible, with plenty of ball chasing and game playing. The only exceptions to this advice are for dogs with injuries or health problems and young dogs which are still growing, as too much exercise can damage their joints. Otherwise, build up your exercise regime gradually, and you'll soon find those pounds dropping off – you and the dog!

DID YOU KNOW ... ?
Dogs and humans are the only animals with prostates.

Talk to your vet

An overweight dog is an unhealthy dog, and your vet can be really useful in helping get your podgy pooch back in shape. A good check up will make sure she's generally fit and healthy, and your vet can then discuss the specific ways in which you can start to get the weight off her. He might prescribe a diet dog food, as well as recommending regular weigh-ins to check on her progress and outlining an exercise regime to suit her needs.

DID YOU KNOW ... ?

There is a wide range of commercial dog food on the market today; this ranges from bags of dry kibble, to semi-moist food, to canned dog food.

Dry commercial dog food – the main advantage of this is convenience and cost. Dry kibble can also help with reducing tartar and plaque build-up on your dog's teeth.

Semi-moist food – this is easy to store and does not need to be refrigerated. These foods tend to have a high sugar content, which can make it easy for your dog to overeat.

Canned dog food – this tends to be more expensive and does need refrigeration after opening. There is a higher water content in canned foods which may necessitate more frequent urination in dogs.

If you decide to feed your dog commercial dog food, look for the highest quality dog food you can afford, which contains the most amounts of healthy, digestible food products from the four food groups.

"Old dogs, like old shoes, are comfortable. They might be a bit out of shape and a little worn around the edges, but they fit well.

Bonnie Wilcox

One foot
in the kennel

chapter 8
One foot in the kennel

Old age creeps up on everyone eventually, and of course our dogs are no exception. With their life crammed into a much shorter span than ours, their ageing process can sometimes feel very quick to us – one day he's a lively puppy and then all of a sudden he's got a grey muzzle and arthritic legs. But old age doesn't have to be all bad news for your dog, and here are some of my top tips for keeping that ageing dog looking—and feeling—in his prime!

What age is old for a dog?

This is a tricky question, as different dogs tend to age at different rates. The first thing to say is that the well-known formula of one dog year being equal to seven human years is no use at all. The best way to work out your dog's human age is by following one of these formulae:

- For little dogs up to 10kg (22lbs) – 12 human years per dog year for the first two years, and then 4 per year thereafter. A 10 year old terrier will be 56 and a 15 year old will be 76.

- For medium dogs 10–30kg (22–66lbs) – 10 human years per dog year for the first two years, and then 5 per year thereafter. A 10 year old spaniel, for example, will be 60 and a 15 year old will be 85.

- For big dogs 30kg (66lbs) + – A bit simpler – 8 human years per dog year all the way. So an 8 year old German Shepherd will be roughly 64 in human terms.

Keep him comfy!

However old your ageing dog is in human terms, there's no doubt she'll appreciate a comfy bed, as older dogs are often prone to aches and pains, especially when the weather is cold and wet. So to make sure your ageing dog is as comfortable as possible, think about upgrading her bed and positioning it somewhere that is totally draft-free and nice and cosy. You can buy a top quality pet bed from your local pet shop, or, if you want to save some money, why not try a little lateral thinking?

One clever idea is to buy a cheap 'egg-crate' foam mattress, cut it in half and place one half on top of the other to give a thick, smooth mattress which you can then cover in a washable fabric. Or for a really big dog, why not drag that old inflatable camping mattress out of the garage and cover it in a thick blanket — as long as she doesn't chew a hole in it, it will make a super soft bed for her!

Quick tip

MEALS ON WHEELS
One of the most important things about looking after an older dog is to get their diet right. Too rich a diet will lead to weight problems and can also cause more serious internal problems such as kidney damage and even diabetes. The ideal thing to do is to feed a high quality natural diet which is not too high in protein or energy, and supplement this with some tasty, healthy home-cooked meals of chicken, rice and vegetables.

Cup of tea and a biscuit?
It's time for a blood test!

As your dog gets older, he might continue to look fit and healthy on the outside, but this isn't always the whole story. Internally, things can be starting to go wrong, and if left unchecked, these underlying problems can suddenly turn into full-blown, life-threatening illnesses. In order to combat these internal problems, which can include kidney disease, liver disease, cancer and diabetes, you need to find them before they become obvious, by which time it's often too late. When your dog reaches middle age (perhaps 50 in human terms), ask your vet for a general blood test. This will check all your dog's internal systems and will either give him a clean bill of health – or enable you to tackle any problems that exist. Repeat these tests every few years as he enters old age to make sure nothing is missed.

Regular exercise is a great way of keeping him young

As your dog gets older he'll probably get a bit slower and less keen to go racing off after squirrels and rabbits. This doesn't mean that he's not enjoying his walks though – just that he's taking life at a slightly slower pace. The best way to keep an older dog fit and happy is to make sure he gets plenty of regular walks, but keep them fairly short and try to make sure he doesn't overdo it. Keep ball throwing and stick chasing to a minimum as this puts a lot of stress on the joints and heart, and concentrate on quiet rambles in the countryside or park.

Have a listen to this …

Sharp hearing is important for all dogs, domestic or wild. Dogs are able to hear sounds that we cannot. Their super-sensitive ears respond both to lower volumes and higher pitched sounds. Have you ever seen a dog prick up its ears? Dog ears are more mobile than ours are, and a dog can adjust them to maximize reception. Eighteen or more muscles tilt, raise and rotate a dog's ears for the best possible sound reception.

The shape of a dog's ears helps with hearing too. Just as we cup our hands around our ears so we can hear better, a dog's upright, curved ears help direct and amplify sound. Erect ears, like those of wild dogs, hear better than the floppy ears of many domestic breeds.

Dogs hear higher frequency sounds than humans although not quite as high as cats can. Frequency, the number of sound wave cycles every second, is measured in a unit called Hertz (Hz). The higher the frequency, the more sound waves per second, the higher pitched the sound.

Dogs' excellent hearing was probably one of the first reasons we tolerated wolves and early dogs near our camps. For centuries we have used them as sentries and guards, alerting us to possible danger. This is especially important at night when it's hard for us to see.

Teach an old dog a new trick!

Here's a great way to rekindle the spark of life in your old dog
– take her to a training class and teach her some new tricks.
Don't go for anything too adventurous; just try to teach her
some interesting new tricks or commands such as rolling onto
her back, or covering her eyes with her paws. Use healthy treats
to encourage her when she gets the new trick right, and you'll
soon find that this new focus has put a puppy-like spring back
into her step!

Here's a wheely good idea!

In the worst cases of arthritis, and in some other conditions
affecting the legs, dogs can end up so crippled they can't even
walk. However, this doesn't necessarily have to be the end,
as there is a solution which can work wonders, especially if
it's only the back legs which are affected.

What you need to do is fit your dog with a set of wheels! Now
this might sound crazy, but there are several companies out
there who make special harnesses for dogs which support their
back end above two wheels. The front legs then simply pull the
weak back end around, and the dog carries on as if there's no
problem at all!

Creaky old bones!

Arthritis is one of the most common problems of older dogs, causing pain and immobility to a high proportion of elderly dogs. There are many causes, ranging from badly formed joints (such as hip dysplasia) to simple wear and tear, but whatever the original cause of the problem, there's a lot you can do to help. Here are my top tips for looking after an arthritic dog:

1. Early diagnosis is vital, so look out for the first signs of arthritis, which include stiffness after exercise, reluctance to jump or climb stairs, lameness on one or more legs and general lethargy and depression.

2. Regular short walks are much better than less frequent long periods of exercise.

3. Weight is crucial as every extra pound on your dog's waistline puts extra pressure on the painful joints so try to get that extra weight off with a lower calorie diet.

4. Your vet can prescribe anti-inflammatory drugs which help to reduce swelling and pain.

5. Food supplements and tablets which contain glucosamine and chondritin sulphate (from your vet) help the joints repair themselves and reduce pain.

6. A teaspoon of cod liver oil every day provides a great source of Omega 3 fatty acids and vitamin D, both of which help keep joints and bones healthy.

If a dog will not come to you after having looked you in the face, you should go home and examine your conscience.

Woodrow Wilson

Pardon?

Deafness is another common problem for older dogs, but it rarely causes serious problems — apart from that selective type of deafness that enables dogs to ignore commands out in the park but hear the slightest sound of a tin of dog food being opened from a hundred yards away!

If your dog is starting to lose his hearing, there are a few important tips that will help him—and you—cope with the problem.

- Use sign language as much as possible when giving commands. Get him used to responding to visual signals rather than just verbal commands.

- Thump the floor with your foot to get his attention through the vibrations of the ground.

- Don't surprise him! Make sure you approach him where he can see you, so as not to give him too much of a shock when you touch him.

- Keep him on a lead. If he can't hear you, and goes too far away to see your visual commands, he could easily get lost, so it's best to keep him on a long lead in the park.

- Accept that his hearing will inexplicably improve whenever there's food about!

A sight for old eyes

Along with hearing problems, many old dogs also suffer from problems with their eyes. The most common cause of poor vision and blindness is a cataract, which are opaque areas in the lens of the eye, and can be caused by diabetes, or just by old age. Nowadays cataracts can be removed using an ultrasound probe which dissolves the lens and removes it from the eye, but this isn't suitable for all dogs, and some are just too old to go through a procedure like this. So what else can you do to help your dog if she is losing her sight? Well here are two easy tips which should make her life a lot easier ...

1. **Don't move the furniture**
   Dogs get to know where everything is in the house and can navigate around even if their sight is poor. If you move things around, they will be confused and bump into things!

2. **Exploit her senses**
   Dab a dilute vinegar solution onto sharp corners and new items – this will help her smell the obstacle before she walks into it!

DID YOU KNOW ... ?
At the end of the Beatles' song "A Day in the Life", an ultrasonic whistle, audible only to dogs, was recorded by Paul McCartney for his Shetland sheepdog.

"A good dog never dies. He stays. He walks besides you on crisp autumn days when frost is on the fields and winter's drawing near. His head is within our hand in his old way."

Mary Carolyn Davies

Doggie disasters!

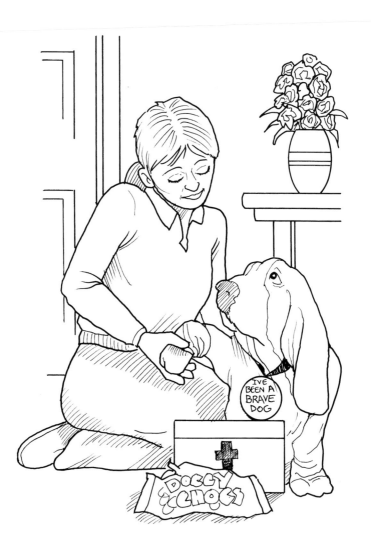

chapter 8
Doggy disasters!

Knowing what to do in case of an emergency or accident involving your dog is a really good idea – and could even save your dog's life. Here are my top tips for those situations when everything goes doggy-shaped and panic starts to set in ...

Don't panic!

Easier said than done I know, but still one of the most important pieces of advice there is. In any emergency situation, you will be far better able to help your dog if you try to remain calm and assess the situation rationally. If you're confronted with an emergency situation and panic sets in, it's worth taking a couple of deep breaths before making a sensible decision about the best course of action. Dogs are very good at picking up emotions from you, and a hysterical owner will not help the dog stay calm and cope with whatever the situation is.

DID YOU KNOW ... ?
Dogs have about 100 different facial expressions, most of them made with the ears. Unfortunately, the likes of bulldogs and pit bulls only have ten, due to their breeding. Therefore, these dogs easily get misinterpreted by other dogs and often get into fights.

---

7 First aid essentials

- Know your vet's emergency number so you can call for advice anytime of the day or night – best to keep it in your mobile phone.

- Find out where you will need to take you dog in an emergency out of normal working hours – many vets are covered by different practices at night and you need to know how to get there in an emergency.

- Keep a basic first aid kit at home and in the car, with bandages and antiseptic cream.

- Always have a supply of fresh water available when you're out and about, especially in hot weather when it can be a life-saver for an over-heating dog.

- Keep a thick blanket in the car so you can wrap up your dog if he's injured and keep him warm until you get to the vet. It will also help you carry him to and from the car easily and without doing further damage to any injuries.

- Research any problems that particularly affect your breed of dog – for example big dogs like Wolfhounds and Great Danes are prone to bloat and twisted stomachs and it's important you know what to look for.

- Take out good pet insurance so that money never becomes an obstacle to treatment.

Sacrifice your socks!

This might sound like a bit of a strange tip for an emergency situation but bear with me and all will become clear!

One of the most common emergency situations faced by dog owners is the cut pad or paw. A sharp piece of glass or metal in the undergrowth can easily cause a deep and nasty cut, and when dog's paws are cut, they tend to bleed an awful lot!

In a situation like this you have got two main priorities. Firstly you need to try to stop the bleeding as much as you can—and this is where the socks come in—and secondly you need to get to your vet a.s.a.p.

To get the bleeding under control, take off both of your socks. Pull one over the bleeding paw, and then use the other to tie the first sock securely in place. If possible, pass the second sock around the area where the cut is so that it applies firm direct pressure to the wound. Then give your vet a ring to let them know you are on your way, and get straight down there without delay.

Quick tip

VINEGAR FOR WASP STINGS
Unlike bees which have an acidic sting, wasp's stings are alkaline, so to neutralise them, dab some vinegar over the swollen area. You can tell that a sting was caused by a wasp and not a bee because wasps don't leave their sting behind.

Bicarbonate of soda for bee stings

In the summer lots of dogs end up with bee stings, especially around the mouth after they chase and try to swallow a bee. The resulting sting can be very painful and cause a big swelling of the lips and face.

However, a simple sting doesn't have to turn into a crisis. If you know that a bee was to blame (either you saw the bee, or you can spot the sting embedded in the dog's mouth) then head to the kitchen and find some bicarbonate of soda. Rub a small amount over the swollen area, and this will reduce the acidity of the sting and help to bring down the swelling.

Snakes in the grass

Snake bites are uncommon in dogs, but do occur. In the UK, the adder is the only poisonous snake, and their bites generally occur around the face of dogs that have been rooting around in undergrowth and disturbed an adder.

Symptoms of a bite usually include a rapid and painful swelling localised around two small puncture marks, and more serious complications are very uncommon. The best course of action is to keep the dog as quiet as possible and take him to your vet as quickly as possible, where a strong anti-inflammatory injection will usually sort out the problem.

In countries where more venomous snakes exist, it is important to immobilise the bite site to prevent the toxin spreading, especially if it is on a limb, and get veterinary assistance as soon as possible.

Dogfight

You're walking your dog on a lead in the park, minding your own business, when all of a sudden, in a flash of black and tan, another dog races up and launches its teeth into your dog's neck. You panic, and try desperately to pull the attacker off but to no avail.

Situations like this are not uncommon and can be very distressing for dog and owner alike. But what can you do to help? Well here are a few important dos and don'ts for breaking up a dog fight:

- Screaming and shouting won't help!

- Never get anywhere near the biting end of either dog – in the heat of battle even your own dog might inadvertently bite you.

- The best technique is to grab the dogs by their back legs, lift them up like a wheelbarrow, and pull them apart.

- If you are on your own, loop a lead around the back legs of one dog and tie it to a solid object like a tree or fence. Then move around to the second dog, and pull him away by the back legs.

- Make sure you secure both dogs before letting go of the legs – otherwise they'll be straight back at each other.

Stop, look and listen!

Cars are one of the biggest killers of dogs. Every day, dogs are killed and injured as they run out in front of cars and are knocked down. Of course, the best thing is to prevent your dog from being at risk. Make sure she's always on the lead whenever you're near a busy road, no matter how well behaved you think she is; and check the security of your garden to make sure she can never escape and end up wandering onto a road.

If the worst does happen though, there are a few important things to remember which could help save your dog's life:

- Firstly, make sure she is safe from further injury. If she's lying in the road, carry her gently to the verge and make her comfortable there.

- Secondly, identify and stop any obvious bleeding by applying direct pressure through a rolled up t-shirt or other item of clothing.

- And finally, get her to your own vet straight away (or emergency vet if it is out of hours), as they will be able to assess her injuries and get her treated straight away.

When sticks get stuck …

You throw a stick for the dog and when he comes back there's something wrong – he can't close his mouth properly and he's constantly pawing at his face in obvious distress. Has he been bitten or stung? Or even run into a tree in his excitement?

The answer is almost certainly not – and the solution to his problem can be easily found if you take a look inside his mouth. What you'll probably find is a piece of stick wedged between his teeth at the top of his mouth. This is quite a common problem, caused when an over-enthusiastic dog races onto a stick and it breaks off in his mouth.

The solution requires a bit of lateral thinking … and a toolkit! Dig out a pair of pliers from the car or garage, and grab hold of the offending stick. Then twist the stick sideways to loosen it from the teeth, and hey presto, it should pop out without too much difficulty!

Cotton wool can save lives

This might sound a bit unlikely, but cotton wool really can be a life-saver, and not just as part of a bandage or dressing. Cotton wool is great for dealing with one of the trickiest emergencies around – the dog who has eaten glass or another sharp item such as a needle.

It works by passing through the digestive system, picking up any sharp objects on the way, and then wrapping them up safely in the fibres of the wool so they pass out the other end without causing serious damage.

The only problem is persuading your dog to eat cotton wool – but there is a good tip which can help overcome this. The thing to do is to tear a few cotton wool balls into small pieces and then soak them in thick cream. Your dog should wolf these down, and within a few days everything should pass though safely.

Diarrhoea!

Diarrhoea is a really common problem in dogs, and it can be caused by lots of things including bacterial infections, bowel inflammation and food allergies. Here are my tips for dealing with this unpleasant problem!

1. If there's a mess in the house, clean it up well using strong disinfectant. Make sure you wash your hands well afterwards and keep children away from the scene of the crime!

2. No food. In mild cases a 12 hour fast should do the trick, but generally 24 hours is best.

3. Plenty of water. Don't ever withhold water as dehydration is the real worry with diarrhoea.

4. Make an electrolyte replacement solution. If the diarrhoea continues for more than a few days, make up a pint of warm water with a teaspoon of salt and a tablespoon of sugar mixed in. Offer this instead of water as it will help replace all the essential electrolytes being lost in the diarrhoea.

5. Boiled chicken and rice. When you reintroduce food after starving him, cook up something really easy to digest like chicken breast and brown rice. Gradually change back to his old food over the next few days if all is well.

6. Yoghurt. Give natural live yoghurt once he's starting to eat again. The probiotics produced by the yoghurt bacteria can help your dog's intestines to recover more quickly.

7. If in doubt – go to the vet. Diarrhoea can be a really serious problem, especially in old or very young dogs, so err on the side of caution and get a veterinary opinion if things aren't getting better.

Vomiting

Being sick can be a sign of serious ill health – but it can also be perfectly normal for lots of dogs. I've known many dogs who would regularly bring back their dinner every now and then (and then proceed to wolf it down again of course!) so you shouldn't worry if your dog develops a similar habit. It's generally caused by over-eating or eating too quickly, and if you want to stop it, try feeding smaller meals more frequently. On the other hand though, persistent vomiting can be a sign of serious problems, and if your dog suddenly starts being sick it's important to get to the vet for a check up as soon as possible.

Big dog + Big meal + Big walk = Big trouble!

One of the most serious and quickly life-threatening canine emergencies is bloat caused by a twisted stomach. As the title to this tip suggests, this is mainly a problem of big dogs like German Shepherds and Great Danes, and it tends to occur after they've eaten a big meal and then had some vigorous exercise. What happens is the stomach twists around and then becomes massively bloated with gas. If not treated very quickly, this can lead to fatal complications, so it's really important to recognise the signs and get veterinary help as soon as possible if you suspect this condition. The main things to look out for are:

- Hard, bloated stomach.
- Vomiting and retching up white froth.
- Pain and discomfort.

The best tips for preventing the problem occurring in the first place are to feed at least twice a day rather than in one big meal, and to avoid any exercise within two hours of a meal.

A remedy for success

Not all doggy disasters are real emergencies. Sometimes it's just a case of stress that's causing problems, and in these cases, there's nothing better than a few drops of good old Rescue Remedy.

Rescue Remedy is a mix of five herbs which was first formulated 70 years ago by a Dr Bach as a treatment for stress in people. Nowadays its well documented effects have been shown to work for dogs as well as people, and so it's well worth having on standby if you're about to move house, or there's another stressful situation coming up.

To use it, just pop a couple of drops on your dog's tongue or in her water and she should be relaxed and stress free for several hours.

Quick tip

ALOE VERA FOR STINGS, CUTS AND GRAZES
Most people know Aloe Vera for its skin soothing properties in people – it can be found in lots of skin products, and there is real scientific evidence to back up the claims that it actually can help skin healing. So why not use it on your dog as well? Aloe Vera gel or cream is great for grazes, cuts and stings because it promotes rapid healing and soothes the pain of damaged skin.

" For me a house
or an apartment
becomes a home
when you add
one set of four legs,
a happy tail, and
that indescribable
measure of love
that we call a dog. "

Roger Caras

The Blue Cross – Britain's Pet Charity

The Blue Cross has been providing practical support, information and advice for pet and horse owners for over 100 years. Through a network of 11 animal adoption centres it re-homes thousands of dogs, cats, small animals and horses every year. Many of the animals taken in by the charity are unwanted, some are strays and a few are much-loved pets whose owners have passed away. Whatever the animal's background, The Blue Cross works hard to match each animal to the right owner, resulting in permanent loving homes.

The charity also has four animal hospitals that provide veterinary treatment for the pets of people who cannot afford private vets' fees. Two equine centres rehabilitate horses before finding them suitable homes on a loan scheme, and the charity's third equine centre will open in 2006.

The Blue Cross receives no government funding and so relies entirely on donations from the public. It has a growing nationwide network of trained volunteers, who speak to classes of children in primary schools and in youth groups. The speakers teach the children empathy, interaction with and behaviour around animals. The Blue Cross also provides the Pet Bereavement Support Service (PBSS), where experienced volunteers give support to those dealing with the loss of a pet.

To find out more about the charity, including animals for adoption, the programme of fundraising events and how to volunteer, please visit **www.bluecross.org.uk**, call 01993 825500, or email info@bluecross.org.uk.

Missing Pets Bureau

Did you know 2,500 dogs go missing in Britain every week, and increasing numbers are now being stolen? To prevent this happening, it is a good idea to have dogs registered with a pet reunification service. The Missing Pets Bureau has nearly 100,000 pets registered nationwide and is the UK's leading pet reunification service. With dog-napping on the rise that extra security, and peace of mind, is worth having!

With the service, you get a unique Petback ID tag linked to specialist support services open 24 hours a day, 365 days a year. If dogs go missing—even on Christmas Day—the team will work day and night to get them back, placing their details on the national Missing Pets Register and putting word out among a network of 12,000 pet care organisations nationwide.

Anyone finding your dog will contact the Missing Pets Bureau using the freephone number on the back of you dog's Petback ID tag and The Missing Pets Bureau will contact you using one of four numbers – including an emergency number. This not only protects your identity – which is essential in the event of dog theft – but also ensures a safe, speedy recovery of your loved one.

There are two types of protection you can go for: Petback Protect or Petback MedAlert. The MedAlert service has the added benefits of DNA identification (which is also vital in the event of dog theft) and further assistance if your dog has been involved in an accident while missing. Don't lose a loved one! Call The Missing Pets Bureau today on freephone 0800 0195 123 or visit their website at **www.missingpetsbureau.com**.

"No one appreciates the very special genius of your conversation as the dog does."

Christopher Morley

Dog
horoscopes

ARIES – Leader of the Pack

(March 21 – April 20)

Traits: Brave, Courageous

Your Aries dog has the tendency to be the leader of the pack. He is adventurous and energetic by nature, always ready for escapades. His confidence and impulsiveness might even get him into precarious situations! His pioneering nature lets him convulsive explore new areas – your shopping bag, or your neighbour's garage. The Aries dog wants to be the one and only dog in a household, and the pride of the neighbourhood. Lack of attention will put him in a bad mood. This dog needs an action-oriented, fun-filled day of play. Obedience and good behaviour are not his favourite games. Be benevolent; do not spoil him too much.

TAURUS – Strong and Silent

(April 21 – May 21)

Traits: Easy-going, Loves Food

Your Taurus dog is a huge softie. He is loving and cuddly. Everybody adores his kind nature. Your Taurus dog is a quiet, loyal, and faithful companion. He does not enjoy exercise, rush and activity. But, he loves lounging around, or a nap in his cosy bed Pampering and patting your Taurus dog is mandatory! Taurus dogs are patient and reliable, special with kids. They want a regular daily routine and feel most comfortable in a secure, peaceful home. Although unlikely to fight, if sufficiently provoked they never give up. Try not to let this happen. Your Taurus dog adores food. Therefore, avoid over-feeding him. Finally, try to understand him; he is not stubborn – he is just lazy!

GEMINI – The Show Off

(May 21 – June 20)

Traits: Enthusiastic, Curious, Entertaining

Your Gemini dog really tries to be a good dog. Just sometimes, his curiosity and keen power let him forget the rules. He loves to communicate with others by eye contact, intense body language, or well-intentioned sounds. Your Gemini dog loves to show off, and provides you endless hours of fun. Teaching him many tricks will help you to keep his restlessness under control. This energetic, innovative dog gets bored quickly, so avoid monotone routines. Be prepared for anything with this dog! Walk your Gemini dog in different surroundings; take him to the swimming pool, the shopping centre, a camping trip. He will easily get accustomed to new environments. Gemini dogs love big families.

CANCER – The Home Lover

(June 22 – July 23)

Traits: Sensitivite, Caring

Highly emotional and intuitive, your Cancer dog knows how you feel, or what you want. The Cancer dog is the most sensitive of all signs. However, this perfect house sitter can be a bit moody and aloof at times. Possessively he will protect you, your children, and your environment. So, warn the postman and strangers! Do not yell at your Cancer dog. Avoid any family upsets or emotional distress. This sympathetic, tender dog would not fare well as a result. Your cancer dog enjoys the comfort of a tranquil home. He does not need outside adventures. He is happy when playing with the kids or sitting in your lap. This dog needs to be with you! Left alone at home he feels unsettled, and uncomfortable.

LEO – The Boss Dog

(July 23 – August 22)

Traits: Assertive, Expressive

The Leo dog deserves respect. Your dog's demanding nature puts him constantly in the centre of the family's attention. Assumingly he waits for fresh and tasty food, regular grooming, and patting. He enjoys being the king of all. He is extremely affectionate, faithful, confident, and proud. Your Leo dog is fiercely loyal, and cannot endure it if you ignore him. He needs attention, praise, and adoration. But, let him earn it; do not provide it for free. Give lot of attention during a training session, praise him for fulfilling a task. So you will not to loose your alpha status. Leo dogs are excellent working dogs. They need a job and appropriate exercise.

VIRGO – The Helper

(August 24 – September 23)

Traits: Diligent, Clean, Reliable

Your Virgo dog is loyal and attentive and expects the same trustworthiness from you. He loves routine and all things in order. So, be on time for feeding and walking him. Virgo dogs are the cleanest and most orderly of all dogs. While alone, they can spend hours for grooming their coat. There will be never horrendous surprises when you return home. Is your Virgo dog humble, with a natural shyness? Then give him a task, and he will work from dawn to dusk, enjoying being helpful and valuable. Virgo Dogs are the best herding dogs and working dogs. They get pleasure from doing the same thing over and over again. Virgo dogs are prone to intestinal problems. They can be fussy, choosy eaters. Feed him only fresh, delicious food. It will be worth the extra money.

LIBRA – The Socialiser

(September 24 – October 23)

Traits: Attractive, Tender

Your Libra dog wants to be everybody's friend. He is charming, easygoing, and sociable. Your Libra dog needs a large social circle, peace, and harmony. Libra dogs enjoy looking nice, and need plenty of attention. They love to be dressed up with exclusive collars and clothes after their daily brushing. Your Libra dog does not want to be on his own! If left alone for long periods, he will start howling, whining, and crying. So, take him with you, even on the short walk to the shop, he really wants to make the trip with you! Exercise is important, because Libra dogs love to eat and gain weight very easily. Libra dogs are happy in large families, and will provide an equal amount of attention to each family member.

SCORPIO – The Cat's Pyjamas

(October 24 – November 22)

Traits: Emotional, Intuitive, Loyal

Your Libra dog wants to be everybody's friend. He is charming, easygoing, and sociable. Your Libra dog needs a large social circle, peace, and harmony. Libra dogs enjoy looking nice, and need plenty of attention. They love to be dressed up with exclusive collars and clothes after their daily brushing. Your Libra dog does not want to be on his own! If left alone for long periods, he will start howling, whining, and crying. So, take him with you, even on the short walk to the shop, he really wants to make the trip with you! However, exercise is important, because Libra dogs love to eat and they gain weight very easily. Libra dogs are happy in large families, and will provide an equal amount of attention to each family member.

SAGITTARIUS – The Happy Dog

(November 23 – December 21)

Traits: Explorer, Hunter

Your Sagittarius dog will make you smile, whenever you are sad. His amusing character will enlighten your day. He is active, trustworthy, and reliable. Your dog is happy by nature, loves to play and jump around in the field. He is an outdoor dog that needs plenty of exercise and a lot space to roam off the lead! This bundle of energy wants to explore the surroundings, catch rats, or chase birds. A farm would be the perfect environment for him. If you live in a city, provide him plenty of time in the park. Always take your Sagittarius dog with you on journeys. This ideal travel companion will really enhance your trip.

CAPRICORN – The Well-Behaved One

(December 22 – January 20)

Traits: Patient, Well behaved

Your Capricorn dog might be loath to exercise, he does not need to run and romp. What he enjoys is a real job. He wants to feel needed. Pulling a sledge, finding your keys, or protecting your children makes him really happy. He will wait patiently until you give him a task. Your Capricorn dog can amuse himself by watching your daily family routine. He is a disciplined, dedicated member of the pack. This dog will be fine alone at home, while you have to go out. He will remain well behaved whilst he waits for your return. An immaculate member of the family who never puts a paw out of place.Capricorn dogs require kindness, warmth, and harmony. More deliberate than other signs, they can reach a ripe old age.

AQUARIUS – The Wacky Dog

(January 20 – February 19)

Traits: Gentle, Individual, Wacky

Keeping your Aquarius dog happy is a challenge. He is definitely not boring or average. None of your neighbour dogs will exhibit such individuality. Your Aquarius dog does not need cuddling, grooming, or sitting in your lap. This smart rebel wants to keep you surprised and excited. He is an affectionate, sociable, and amusing companion. This independent and inventive dog has his own rules. He learns very fast, but will do things only when he wants to do it so don't force or bother him. Provide him the freedom he needs to express himself. Your Aquarius dog has no serious behaviour problems. He loves people and other pets. His eccentric nature helps you to keep your sense of humour.

PISCES – The Perceptive Dog

(February 20 – March 20)

Traits: Qiet, Gentle, Perceptive

Your Pisces Dog is a sensitive, adaptable, and intuitive dog. He is calm and peace loving. He feels most comfortable in a quiet, tranquil environment. This sweet, sympathetic mummy dog just wants to please you. Your Pisces dog does not need a big garden. He wants to be close to you. It makes him happy to follow you like a shadow. The acute intuition of the Pisces dog can sense when you are sick or upset and will sit beside you to make you feel better. Because of his caring nature and noble character, he gets a lot of sympathy and rewards. Pisces dogs are excellent swimmers. They love water and will jump in every puddle. Their favourite living place would be near a lake, or close to the beach.

" If you can look at
a dog and not feel
vicarious excitement
and affection, you
must be a cat. "

Anon

Healthy recipes
for your dog

Chicken & rice

*Let's start with something really easy – and very healthy.
It combines one of the healthiest proteins available—chicken
—with rice which is an easily digestible carbohydrate, and
a mixture of veg which provide lots of vitamins and minerals.
It's great for all dogs, including those with sensitive digestions
and older dogs. It's ideal for freezing, so you can store it
in single-serving sized bags, then simply defrost a tasty
and healthy meal the next time you want to give your dog
something special.*

Makes a couple of medium dog sized portions.

225g (8oz) chicken mince
200g (7oz) rice (preferably brown)
1 small carrot, finely grated

150g (5oz) fresh peas
1 teaspoon Marmite

- Boil the rice in a large pan of boiling water. When the
  rice is almost cooked (1–2 minutes away), drop the grated
  carrot and peas into the water and let it simmer until the
  rice is done. This makes the veg much more digestible,
  without losing all of its goodness. When the rice is cooked,
  drain well.

- Meanwhile, fry the mince for a few minutes until it is
  browned—you shouldn't need to add any oil as there
  is plenty of fat in the mince—and add it to the rice.

- Finally, mix in the yeast extract and serve once cooled.
  Prepare yourself for a slobbery lick of gratitude!

Kidney casserole

There are few things better for your dog to eat every now and then than a bit of kidney. It's packed full of good quality protein, essential fatty acids and loads of vitamins. The only downside is it tastes a bit of wee – but dogs don't seem to mind one little bit! Makes a jumbo dish of casserole.

125g (4oz) stewing steak, diced
2 lambs' kidneys, chopped into quarters
20g (½oz) plain flour
1 teaspoon Marmite
1 tablespoon oil
1 small swede, diced (approx 250g/8oz)
1 small carrot, diced

- Roll the kidneys and diced steak in the flour. Then heat the oil in a large saucepan and stir in the Marmite. Drop the floury meat into the oil, and cook for a few minutes until it's all nice and brown. Then add the diced veg and cook for another couple of minutes.

- Finally, add enough water to cover all the ingredients, put the lid on, turn the heat down, and leave to simmer for about an hour.

- When the dog's patience is finally exhausted and he can wait no more, spoon out the bone and discard it (somewhere where the dog can't get to it!), and let the stew cool down before pouring a generous ladle-full on top of a handful of his normal dried biscuits and serving with a smile!

Meaty parsnip mash

This is one of Jack's all time favourites – and I must admit to being rather partial to a spoonful myself. It's full of real meaty chunks, which dogs love, as well as plenty of veg for vitamins, and cheese for calcium. Not one for the older dog as there's too much rich protein, but ideal for all other dogs.

250g (8oz) stewing steak, diced
1 teaspoon oil
A couple of medium potatoes (around 350g/12oz)
A couple of parsnips (around 200g/7oz)
1 carrot
½ teaspoon Marmite
100g (3½oz) cheddar cheese, grated

- The first step is to get a big pan of water on to boil while you chop up all the veg. Wash them to get rid of any nasty chemicals, but don't peel them as this removes a lot of the goodness. Put all of the veg in together and let it simmer for about 15 minutes – until it's all quite soft.

- Meanwhile, fry up the diced steak in the oil. Don't worry about cooking it all the way through – dogs love rare meat.

- When the veg is done, drain off the water and set about it with a masher until you've got a thick mash in the pan. Then mix in the Marmite, cheese and fried steak. Mix it all together and then let it cool. Serve on its own or mixed in with some dried biscuits.

Liver & bacon chews

In my mind there are few smells as appealing as that of bacon gently crisping in a pan. And it's not just me that thinks like this – Jack, and every dog I've ever known, also loves bacon, which is why these lovely chewy treats are such a winner. They're made of crunchy pieces of bacon in a chewy dough made from liver, egg and flour, and they are brilliant as training bribes. Makes several helpings.

225g (8oz) liver
1 egg
1 cup plain flour

¼ teaspoon oregano
2 rashers bacon

- Fry the bacon until just crisp, and then allow it to cool before cutting up into tiny pieces. Keep the fat from the cooking as you'll need that in a minute.

- Next, put the liver into the blender and whizz until it forms a thick red sludge. Pour in the fat from the frying pan (wait until it has cooled a little), break in the egg and sprinkle in the oregano. Fire up the blender again and continue to mix for a few seconds, until it forms a nice, uniform paste. Then pour it into a large mixing bowl, add in the bacon and mix well.

- Finally, mix in the flour to form a thick dough which you can roll out and divide into grape-sized pieces. Place these on a well-greased baking tray and cook in a moderate oven for half an hour.

Great balls of egg

If you want to have a bit of fun with your dog, these treats are great. They are basically hard balls of oatmeal pastry wrapped around a hardboiled egg, and are designed to keep your dog happy as she chases it around trying to crack it open and get to the tasty egg and cheese centre. The recipe makes 5, but they need to be eaten within a few days, so why not give away a few to doggie-loving friends.

50g (1¾oz) butter or margarine
75g (2½oz) rolled oats
75g (2½oz) plain flour

6 eggs
½ teaspoon Marmite
50g (1¾oz) cheese, grated

- Firstly, hardboil 5 of the six eggs (about 8 minutes is fine) and remove the shells.

- Then to make the crunchy outer, rub the butter, oats and flour together to form a crumbly mix. Beat in the remaining egg, mix in the Marmite and gradually add just enough hot water to make a sticky, but firm, dough. Roll this out thinly on a floury board and cut into five equal squares.

- Now sprinkle a little cheese on each square, and place an egg in the middle of each one. Wrap up the dough to completely enclose the egg and place the finished balls on a well-greased baking tray. Cook for 25 minutes in a moderate oven, allow to cool and let the games begin!

Bacon flapjacks

Flapjacks are one of my personal favourites, and they can also make a good tasty dog treat. They're made mainly of oats, which are one of the best sources of carbohydrate for your dog, as they're high in essential fatty acids, protein and minerals, including the all-important calcium. Makes five balls.

Their usual downside is the high levels of sugar and fat, but I've reduced both in this recipe so it's not too rich – however, I'd still be cautious about offering this to your dog if he's having trouble with his weight, and in general it's definitely a recipe to cook, store, and give in small amounts.

100g (3½oz) margarine
125g (4oz) porridge oats
50g (1¾oz) self-raising flour
2 tablespoons cornflour

1 teaspoon mustard
2 tablespoons olive oil
2 rashers bacon

- Fry the bacon until crispy and, when cool, cut into little pieces. Keep the oil from the pan to hand.

- Meanwhile, mix together the margarine, oats, flour and cornflour in a large bowl. Add in the mustard, chopped bacon and olive oil, mix thoroughly and then press into a greased baking tray. Drizzle the remaining fat in the frying pan over the mixture before putting it into a hot oven (190°C/375°F/Gas 5) for 20 minutes.

Fruit shake

*It might surprise you, but in the wild, dogs would eat quite
a lot of fruit. This comes from eating the remains of other
animals that have themselves eaten fruit, and from picking up
windfalls. It provides a great supply of energy in the form of
readily available fruit sugars, as well as all the vitamins and
antioxidants we associate with fruit.*

*So this recipe, which is stuffed full of the goodness of raw fruit,
is one of the healthiest in the book and the addition of a bit of
yoghurt also adds to its healthy qualities and makes it more
palatable. Some dogs will lap this up on its own, but for the
average, fast-food loving hound, you might need to pour it
over his everyday dinner to get the goodness down him.
Makes several portions.*

1 banana	1 orange
1 apple	1 small pot of yoghurt (125ml/4fl.oz)
A few strawberries	

- Put the peeled banana (watch out where you put the
  skin ...), apple and strawberries into a blender and whiz them
  up until they are well and truly puréed. Pour into a bowl
  and add in the peeled and chopped up orange. Finally, mix
  in the yoghurt and give it a good stir.

- Try this out but if he turns his nose up, you can try either
  pouring it over his dried dog kibbles, or adding half a tin
  of wet meaty dog food to the shake mixture.

Puppy cheesy treats

These tasty biscuits are an ideal treat or snack for a hungry puppy. Use them to help with training by rewarding good behaviour – but make sure you don't overdo them as they are quite rich and fatty. One or two treats a day as part of your training schedule is ideal. Makes enough to last a couple of weeks.

250g (8oz) whole wheat flour
150g (5oz) grated cheddar cheese
50g (1¾oz) butter

1 clove garlic
1 beef stock cube
Milk

- Mix the flour and butter together in a large bowl and run the fat in until it forms a crumbly mixture. Then add in the grated cheese, crushed garlic and crumbled stock cube and mix well.

- Slowly add milk to the mixture until it forms a very sticky dough. Flour your hands and start kneading the dough until it forms a single firm lump. Turn it out onto a floured surface and roll it out to about 1.25cm (½") thick. Cut the dough up into puppy-sized biscuits using a small pastry cutter—or if you don't have one, try using the end of an apple corer —this cuts the dough into just the right sized little rounds.

- Then place the biscuits onto a greased baking tray and cook in a moderate oven (180°C/350°F/Gas 4) for 15–20 minutes, until they are golden brown. Allow to cool and then store in an airtight container.

Pooch pizza

Ideal for a doggy birthday, this tasty pizza is healthy thanks to the layer of spinach which provides iron and vitamins, and the low-fat turkey mince on top. Makes one medium sized dog pizza.

100g (3½oz) dried dog kibble   100g (3½oz) turkey mince
30g (1oz) butter or margarine   50g (1¾oz) plain flour
100g (3½oz) spinach, finely chopped
50g (1¾oz) cheddar cheese, grated

- Firstly you need to grind up the dried biscuits into a fine powder using a blender. Then moisten the kibble powder with enough warm water to make it into a really moist and gooey mess. Leave it to stand for ten minutes, and add more water if you need to, as the kibble absorbs a lot of water.

- Next, add in the flour and slightly melted butter, and mix it all together to form a thick dough. It should firm up into a nice dry ball which you can roll out on a floured surface until it's about ½cm (¼") inch thick.

- For the topping, you need to fry up the turkey mince for five minutes or so and then mix it together with the finely chopped spinach. Cover the base with this mixture and finally, sprinkle on the grated cheese.

- Cook in a moderate oven for 20–25 minutes – until the top is golden brown. Allow to cool thoroughly and then slice into wedges before serving.

Valentine's heart

If the romantic day should come around and there's no one to share it with this year, why not treat the dog to something truly special? It'll certainly bring you love – but perhaps not quite the kind of love you were looking for! Still, a slobbery kiss from the dog is better than nothing!

One lamb's heart	1 leek
1 carrot	100g (3½oz) rice

- Take the heart and cover it with boiling water in a medium sized saucepan (if you want to imagine this as the heart of a jilted lover, feel free!). Add in the chopped carrot and leek and let it all simmer for 15 minutes.

- In the meantime, cook the rice according to the instructions on the packet and allow it to cool down.

- When the heart has finished cooking, drain off the water, and carefully slice it into thin strips. Put the cooked carrot and leek into a blender and reduce them to a thick purée.

- Once everything has cooled down, serve the heart on a bed of rice and top with a spoonful of the vegetable purée. It might not quite be the romantic Valentine's meal you were hoping for, but the dog will love you for making the effort – and you never know, next year might be better!

Steak & kidney burgers

*Normal beef burgers are OK for dogs, but if you want to cook up
something special that the dog will really love—and which is
a lot more healthy for him—try these steak and kidney burgers.
The kidney gives extra flavour, as well as essential nutrients
such as fatty acids, vitamins and iron. Make up a load and put
them in the freezer, so when you have a BBQ, the dog isn't left
out! Makes 10 burgers.*

250g (8oz) lamb's kidneys, finely chopped
250g (8oz) beef mince
1 small carrot, finely grated
2 eggs

- This is another recipe where we're going to use some of the
  egg shell to add calcium to the recipe. Break the eggs into
  a bowl and then put the shells on a baking tray and cook
  them for ten minutes in a moderate oven. This helps to dry
  them out as well as killing off any nasty bugs. Then grind
  them up with a pestle and mortar or rolling pin until they
  form a fine powder.

- While the egg shells are baking, fry the grated carrot for
  five minutes in a small amount of oil. Then mix the mince,
  finely chopped kidney and beaten eggs together, and add
  in the cooked carrot. Sprinkle ½ teaspoon of the egg shell
  powder in and knead the mixture together. Then form it
  into burgers and cook on the BBQ just as you would with
  a normal burger. Allow to cool and then serve to the dog
  with some rice or pasta.

Pasta with chicken & spinach

A quick and easy recipe guaranteed to have you and the dog salivating with anticipation. It's really healthy (for you too) so you can feed this as often as you want – and it's ideal for older dogs as well. Makes enough for you and the dog.

250g (8oz) pasta (any shape)
1 teaspoon olive oil
100g (3½oz) cooked chicken breast
100g (3½oz) spinach, shredded
150ml (5fl.oz) fromage frais
1 clove garlic, crushed
50g (1¾oz) parmesan cheese, flaked

- Cook the pasta in a large pan of boiling water until just tender. Drain and return to the pan.

- Meanwhile, beak the chicken into small pieces and gently fry with the garlic in the oil for five minutes until crispy and brown. Add in the shredded spinach and continue cooking for a couple of minutes until it has reduced down. Then pour in the fromage frais and cook until the sauce is hot through.

- Pour the chicken sauce over the pasta, add half the parmesan and toss to mix thoroughly. Sprinkle on the remaining parmesan and serve – hot for you, and cold for the dog.

Sausage & lentil casserole

A great dish for you and the dog to share on a cold winter's evening after a long walk. Lentils are not a bad food for dogs, but they are not totally nutritionally balanced (and can cause wind!) so this is a dish best fed occasionally rather than every day. Reserve it for a particularly wet and cold evening when you both need cheering up with something warm and tasty. Makes enough for you, the dog and friends.

6 sausages
1 teaspoon olive oil
1 small leek, finely chopped
3 tablespoons parsley
Salt and pepper

600ml (20fl.oz) chicken stock
1 teaspoon balsamic vinegar
2 garlic cloves, crushed
150g (5oz) Puy lentils

- Fry the sausages in the olive oil for 7 or 8 minutes until browned all the way around. Then add in the chopped leek and garlic and cook for a further 5 minutes.

- Next, add in the lentils and hot stock. Bring to the boil and simmer gently for 45 minutes, until the lentils are tender and most of the stock has been absorbed.

- Finally, add in the vinegar and chopped parsley, and season with salt and pepper to taste.

- Eat yours while it's still piping hot, but make the dog wait until it has cooled down before spooning out a couple of sausages and sauce into his bowl.

Chicken, spinach & fish mash

Now our dog Jack might not be exactly what you'd call elderly at the moment, but when I was trying out this recipe he absolutely loved it. The combination of the easy-to-digest protein from the chicken, with the good quality carbohydrate from the sweet potato, and the vitamins from the spinach make it super healthy – and the sardines add in essential omega-3 oils as well as a bit of extra taste.

250g (8oz) chicken mince
400g (14oz) sweet potatoes
250g (8oz) spinach, shredded
1 tin sardines in oil
½ teaspoon egg shell powder
or 1x1000mg calcium supplement, crushed.
1 teaspoon brewer's yeast

- Boil the sweet potatoes in their skins until tender (about ten minutes) and then drain and mash them. At the same time, gently fry the chicken mince, until it is cooked through, then add the spinach and cook for a few minutes until reduced.

- Finally, add the sardines, along with all the oil, to the mince and spinach, and mix it all together with the mash in a mixing bowl. Add in the calcium or egg shell, and the brewer's yeast and form into egg-sized balls.

Old dog power juice

There's no doubt that fresh fruit and veg help to keep old age at bay – lots of studies have proved that eating plenty of fruit and veg reduces the risk of all sorts of diseases, including cancer. Getting a dog, especially an old boy, to eat down a plate of fruit and veg is nigh on impossible – which is why I've come up with this cunning recipe for a revitalising juice drink which old dogs will love. Feed this once a week and you'll keep him fighting fit for years to come!

300g (10oz) assorted fruit and veg – anything you have to hand (except onions, tomatoes and mushrooms)
100g (3½oz) chicken liver

- Put the liver in a small bowl and pour over just enough boiling water to cover. Let it stand for ten minutes.

- Meanwhile, chuck all the veg and fruit into the blender. Anything goes here—apples, plums, cabbage, courgettes, carrots—as long as it's fruit or veg and it's not an onion, tomato or mushroom, in it goes. Whizz it all up to make a thick purée. Then add in the liver, complete with its water.

- Blend together, adding more water if necessary, until you have a thick drink. Pour a reasonable amount into the dog bowl and watch her slurp it up. You can freeze the rest if you have some left over.

Yoghurt chicken & rice

There are lots of possible causes of diarrhoea, ranging from nasty infections to dietary insensitivities, but the treatment often has one thing in common – a period of starvation (often 24 hours) followed by the use of a really bland diet for a few days. This regime is often sufficient to sort out most mild cases of diarrhoea, and it's a sensible first step to consider rather than rushing to the vet straight away (obviously if this doesn't do the trick, or the dog is really unwell, you should get him straight to the surgery for a proper check over).

This recipe is particularly good because both chicken and rice are very easily digested and unlikely to irritate the bowel, and the live yoghurt provides probiotics which help to restore the correct balance of good bacteria in the gut.

200g (7oz) chicken mince
½ cup of rice (preferably brown)
Plain, live yoghurt

- Add the rice and the mince to a large pan of boiling water. Cooking them together in this way means the flavour of the meat soaks deep into the rice, making it much more palatable (which is important for such a bland meal).

- When the rice is cooked, drain away the water and allow the mixture to cool.

  For each serving, mix with a tablespoon of yoghurt (for a Labrador-sized dog).

A
Abby
Abel
Angus
Annie
Archie
Axle

B
Bailey
Blue
Brandy
Bruce
Buddy
Buster

C
Cassie
Charlie
Chelsea
Chip
Chloe
Cody

D
Daisy
Dixie
Duchess
Duke
Dusty
Dylan

E
Ebony
Echo
Edgar
Ellie
Elmer
Emerson

F
Fable
Felix
Fido
Floyd
Frisbee
Fritz

G
Gatsby
Genie
Goldie
Gunner
Gusto
Gypsy

H
Harley
Heidi
Holly
Homer
Honey
Hunter

I
Iggy
Inca
Indigo
Ipod
Iris
Ivy

J
Jack
Jade
Jasmine
Jasper
Jilly
Joker

K
Kaiser
Katie
Kermit
Kiki
Kipling
Kosmo

L
Lady
Laser
Liberty
Limbo
Lucky
Lulu

M
Maggie
Maverick
Max
Missie
Molly
Murphy

N
Nacho
Nellie
Newton
Ninja
Nudge
Nutmeg

O
Ollie
Orbit
Orion
Oscar
Otis
Ozzie

P
Paisley
Patsy
Petra
Phoenix
Pickles
Princess

Q
Quasi
Queenie
Quiche
Quicksilver
Quincy
Quirky

R
Rambo
Rebel
Rocky
Rolly
Roxanne
Rusty

S
Sadie
Sam
Sandy
Sasha
Scoobie
Sparky

T
Tango
Tasha
Texas
Toby
Trixie
Trouper

U
Ulysses
Uma
Urchin
Ursa
Ursula
Utopia

V
Velvet
Vince
Vinny
Violet
Vixen
Voodoo

W
Wanda
Wellington
Whiskey
Willow
Winston
Woody

X
Xanadu
Xanthus
Xavier
Xena
Xerox
Xray

Y
Yabba
Yahoo
Yankee
Yogi
Yo-Yo
Yummy

Z
Zelda
Zeus
Ziggy
Zipper
Zodiac
Zorro

My tips

Index

'The Greatest Tips in the World' books

Baby & Toddler Tips
by Vicky Burford
ISBN 978-1-905151-70-7

Barbeque Tips
by Raymond van Rijk
ISBN 978-1-905151-68-4

Cat Tips by Joe Inglis
ISBN 978-1-905151-66-0

Cookery Tips
by Peter Osborne
ISBN 978-1-905151-64-6

Cricketing Tips
by R. Rotherham & G. Clifford
ISBN 978-1-905151-18-9

DIY Tips
by Chris Jones & Brian Lee
ISBN 978-1-905151-62-2

Dog Tips by Joe Inglis
ISBN 978-1-905151-67-7

Etiquette & Dining Tips
by Prof. R. Rotherham
ISBN 978-1-905151-21-9

Freelance Writing Tips
by Linda Jones
ISBN 978-1-905151-17-2

Gardening Tips
by Steve Brookes
ISBN 978-1-905151-60-8

Genealogy Tips
by M. Vincent-Northam
ISBN 978-1-905151-72-1

Golfing Tips
by John Cook
ISBN 978-1-905151-63-9

Horse & Pony Tips
by Joanne Bednall
ISBN 978-1-905151-19-6

Household Tips
by Vicky Burford
ISBN 978-1-905151-61-5

Personal Success Tips
by Brian Larcher
ISBN 978-1-905151-71-4

Podcasting Tips
by Malcolm Boyden
ISBN 978-1-905151-75-2

Property Developing Tips
by F. Morgan & P Morgan
ISBN 978-1-905151-69-1

Retirement Tips
by Tony Rossiter
ISBN 978-1-905151-28-8

Sex Tips
by Julie Peasgood
ISBN 978-1-905151-74-5

Travel Tips
by Simon Worsfold
ISBN 978-1-905151-73-8

Yoga Tips
by D. Gellineau & D. Robson
ISBN 978-1-905151-65-3

Pet Recipe books

The Greatest Feline Feasts in the World by Joe Inglis
ISBN 978-1-905151-50-9

The Greatest Doggie Dinners in the World by Joe Inglis
ISBN 978-1-905151-51-6

'The Greatest in the World' DVDs

The Greatest in the World – Gardening Tips
presented by Steve Brookes

The Greatest in the World – Yoga Tips
presented by David Gellineau and David Robson

The Greatest in the World – Cat & Kitten Tips
presented by Joe Inglis

The Greatest in the World – Dog & Puppy Tips
presented by Joe Inglis

For more information about currently available
and forthcoming book and DVD titles please visit:

www.thegreatestintheworld.com

or write to:

The Greatest in the World Ltd
PO Box 3182
Stratford-upon-Avon
Warwickshire CV37 7XW
United Kingdom

Tel / Fax: +44(0)1789 299616
Email: info@thegreatestintheworld.com

The author

Since starring in the hit BBC 1 series 'Vets in Practice', Joe Inglis has managed to juggle the demands of being a vet with a blossoming and diverse media career. This has included presenting roles in many television programmes, most notably Blue Peter, as well as writing books, and contributing to magazines and newspapers.

Joe qualified as a veterinary surgeon from Bristol University in 1996 and he attributes his passion for the natural world and great spirit of adventure to being a direct descendent of Charles Darwin — his great-great-great-grandson to be precise!